SOUTHAMPTON'S
LOST STREETS
St Mary's and Golden Grove

SOUTHAMPTON'S LOST STREETS

St Mary's and Golden Grove

DAVE MARDEN

First published 2019 by DB Publishing, an imprint of JMD Media Ltd, Nottingham, United Kingdom.

ISBN 978-1-78091-587-6

Printed in the UK

Contents

Acknowledgements

The content of this book is greatly reliant upon the many images displaying the houses and streets that were dutifully recorded by the Southampton Council prior to the clearance programmes of the 1950s and 1960s. I am sincerely grateful to have been given permission to use their extensive archive. In doing so, I have downloaded many images from the City Archives PortCities website and, while it will be appreciated these are of low resolution, I have done my best to enhance them to a useable standard and, although they may not be pin sharp, I feel they are of sufficient quality to portray the streets and buildings as they were. Unless otherwise credited, all images are from that source, but if I have inadvertently infringed anyone's copyright I offer my sincere apologies.

In the course of my research I am grateful once again to references in:

PortCities website
Sotonopedia.wikidot.com
Southampton's Inns and Taverns by the late Tony Gallaher

Introduction

In my earlier book *Southampton's Chapel Area – A Hundred Years of the Past*, I wrote about the district of Chapel and its contribution towards the growth of the docks and its shipping lines, but those who lived in St Mary's and Golden Grove were equally invaluable in providing the workforce essential to the town's prosperity, and this book looks at the growth of the area over a period of just over a century – from the 1840s through to when it all disappeared. I have had great pleasure in compiling this second volume illustrating the old streets of downtown Southampton, many of which I can remember still standing before the mass clearance programmes.

Dear old Chapel no longer exists and its neighbours, St Mary's and Golden Grove, had also been obliterated by the late 1950s and early 1960s, Bevois, Cumberland and Grove Streets remain as mere stubs of the substantial roads they once were. Those names that do survive have been rebuilt with modern homes and are completely unrecognisable from their former selves.

Grove Street was a natural entrance from Chapel Road into Golden Grove and the street scene beyond was very similar to its Chapel neighbours, with its busy roads packed with houses, pubs, shops and small industries. I knew many of the old streets from my childhood days, passing through them on my way to school, firstly at Ascupart Junior (now St Mary's) and later to Central Secondary Boys at Argyle Road. I saw many of them gradually disappear, one by one, to be replaced by the modern flats and houses of the Golden Grove estate in the 1960s and 1970s.

Over the years, many books have been written about Southampton's history – and rightly so as it has a rich and colourful past – with many of them focussing on the ancient and medieval periods, and continuing on into the Victorian and Edwardian era, but throughout this time, very little has been written regarding the working-class population and its contribution towards Southampton's growth from a modest spa town to an industrialised city and major port. To house those workers, many streets of tightly packed terrace houses were laid down outside the old town to provide thousands of homes. Innovators, entrepreneurs and wealthy individuals may have built the infrastructure but the workforce was the backbone of the town's success. Although the city's industry has declined in recent years, and the old neighbourhoods bulldozed away, the contribution of the ordinary folk should not be overlooked.

Modern-day planning by developers of housing schemes makes full use of space on any available land, but their Victorian predecessors knew a thing or two about maximising the number of working-class homes they could build on any given plot. Not only did terrace houses and tenements line the old streets, but any available land between them was utilised with dismal yards and courts accessed by narrow alleys where tiny cottages, hidden from public view, at least provided a roof over somebody's head. While most families maintained their terrace homes to a decent standard, those tucked away in the courts and alleys would have struggled to make the most of their environment, when damp and decay often set in to add a sense of squalor. Overcrowding with sometimes two or three families in a small house merely added to the problems, but people were resilient – they had to be as there was no other option.

In my previous book I referred the neighbourliness of families growing up together over several generations. This was also apparent in St Mary's and Golden Grove, something that was sadly lost when redevelopments dispersed those long-established communities to alien territories and new estates on the outskirts of the town.

As ever, difficulties have arisen when trying to identify buildings and their occupants during the various renumbering schemes, where streets developed piecemeal over a number of years and individual groups of buildings all had the same numbers. Tenants could have been in the same house but had several different door numbers over time, and it has only been possible to locate those buildings if the occupants were in the same residence after the change of door number. Also, some of the early street directories and ordnance maps are not always accurate and mistakes are perpetuated in later editions. That said, I hope I have been successful in pinning down most of the buildings and portraying them on the maps I have created as illustrations, together with notes of their more interesting occupants

Once again, I must stress this book is not intended as a definitive record of the area but principally to show what was once there and is now gone. As with Chapel, it is commendable that the (then) town council produced a photographic record of the houses and buildings on so many of the streets before they were cleared. The images now reveal and reflect the past neighbourhoods of those generations that lived there, but sadly many were photographed in a dilapidated state just prior to demolition and perhaps they no longer show the pride and character of the old place that was once prevalent.

This book will hopefully revive the memories of those who lived there, or perhaps enable others to see where past generations of their families grew up. To those who know nothing of the area, I trust it will be an insight to how and where many of its past residents lived.

Dave Marden, 2019

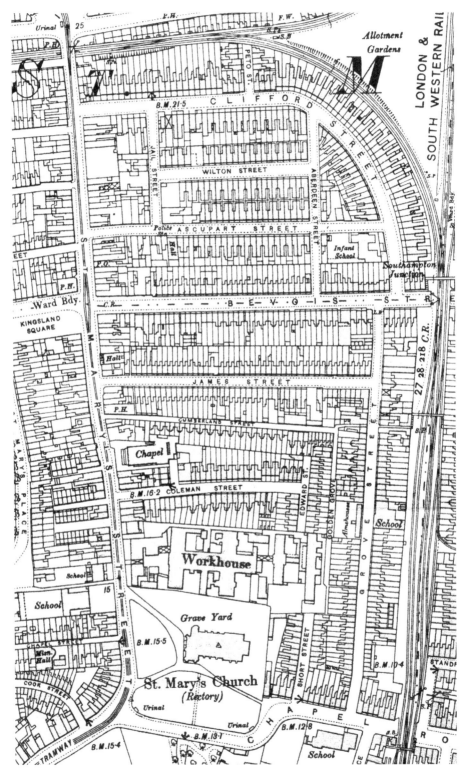

A 1950s aerial view of the streets and terraces that have long since disappeared, with St Mary Street at the bottom right of the picture and Ascupart School (now St Mary's school) can be seen on the left. This whole area was redeveloped as the Golden Grove housing estate in the 1960s and 1970s and the gasworks site at the top left is now rebuilt as St Mary's Stadium.

Chapter 1

West of St Mary Street

Some of Southampton's early Victorian dwellings for the working classes were built off the west side of St Mary Street, and those long-disappeared streets running through to St Mary's Place and Houndwell Place are quite fascinating. Those of the Kingsland area will merit a book of their own, but others such as Church Street and Chapel Street, along with St Mary's and Pope's Buildings, are well worth investigation.

Opposite: The streets St Mary's and Golden Grove as they were in 1908 with the tightly packed terraces that have all since been swept away. The old workhouse is now the City College and St Mary's Church still dominates, but the remainder of the area now lives only in memories of those who knew it.

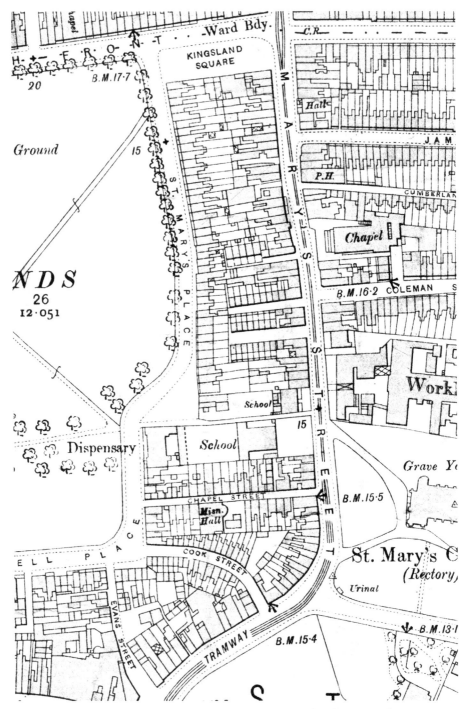

The old buildings west of St Mary Street from Kingsland Square down to Evans Street shown in 1910 where there was a high concentration of early Victorian housing.

14

Church Row and York Square

In the early 1800s, the district at the southern end of St Mary Street between Cook Street and Evans Street was a warren of alleyways leading to several hidden courtyards, the principal ones being Church Row and York Square. Both were surrounded by taller buildings, so daylight must have been quite scarce. On the 1846 Ordnance Survey map, this was a mass of tightly packed buildings, all long since swept away. Cook Street still survives (if only in name), but Evans Street disappeared when the Kingsway dual carriageway was laid down from Six Dials through to Marsh Lane in the 1960s.

This is the probable layout of the dwellings in York Square and Church Row before much of it was cleared in the early 1900s, and both were entirely gone by the mid-1930s.

Nos 2-3 Church Row in what seems to have been a quite miserable environment.

Another of the cottages that made up Church Row.

This photograph is identified as being houses in York Square in the 1930s, but I cannot quite identify its location on the various maps. The tea chest suggests the occupants may already have been packing their possessions prior to demolition.

Church Row (otherwise known as Church Court) was accessed from an alley that ran from between Nos 5 and 6 St Mary Street, which also led through to York Square. There was also access from next to No 16 Evans Street (previously named York Street). Church Row was made up of six dwellings and, in the late 1800s, housed many dock workers and seafarers. York Square originally had 18 homes in total, but Nos 8 to 18 disappeared from the directories in the early 1900s. In the 1890s there were no less than three families associated with the tailoring profession and a Mrs Donnelly was one of the final residents at No 5, having lived there since the early 1900s.

It has been a difficult task to identify the exact locations of those buildings from the directories as their occupants do not seem to have been worthy of inclusion in some of the earlier editions. There is also a

The same houses in York Square seen from the opposite direction.

This view into the courtyard of York Square shows some of the buildings there were three-storeys high.

great disparity between the various maps and the photographic records as to exactly what was where, and the numbered diagram is my best estimate as to how things were. Much of this area, including the courts, was cleared away in the mid-1930s

Cook Street

Cook Street appears on the 1846 map but hardly merits a mention in the street directories until the early 1860s. The crescent of buildings was numbered 1 to 31, but sometimes 2 to 33, until the early 1900s when many of those on the north side disappeared. Nos 19-27 were gone by 1912 and the remainder were removed in the slum clearance of that area in the 1930s.

In some of the early directories, Nos 5 and 6 St Mary Street were listed as Nos 1 and 33 Cook Street. Nos 2-17 were on the south side and housed the usual mixture of labourers, semi-skilled people, tradesmen and seafarers. William Coombes at No 7 was there from at least the 1860s until 1907, working as a warehousman, porter and general labourer. Of

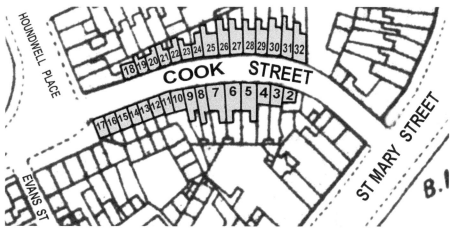

The full compliment of houses in Cook Street as they were in 1908. In some early directories, the buildings on the corners with St Mary Street were included as Nos 1 and 33. Nos 18-27 disappeared in the early 1900s and the remainder were all gone by 1938.

Nos 3-6 Cook Street looking north towards Houndwell Place in 1935.

Another view of Cook Street in 1935, looking south towards St Mary Street from No 17 to No 12, with some of the local children outside No 16.

the families that were in residence when the street came down in 1938, the Jenkins family had been at No 17 from the 1880s, John Henry Willett was at No 3 from the early 1900s, and Edward Herbert Beard and his family were at No 16 at the very end.

On the north side were Nos 18 to 32, but Nos 18 to 27 had been demolished around 1910, and the remainder (Nos 28-32) lasted until the 1930s along with those on the opposite side. Boot maker Henry White plied his trade at No 32 from around 1870 until about 1925. Back in the 1880s, E Spain and Co had a stable yard adjacent to No 32 and this was later occupied by coal merchant William Henry Jerram.

Chapel Street

Chapel Street, opposite St Mary's Churchyard, ran from the bottom of St Mary Street through to Houndwell Place. These days it is a pleasant pedestrian walkway but back in Victorian times it was a typical street of the neighbourhood with a mixture of grim two and three-storey buildings, two pubs and a mission hall, together with a number of narrow alleyways leading off into dismal courtyards. Grace's Court, Newman's Court, Bells Buildings and Bates Court were such groups of buildings

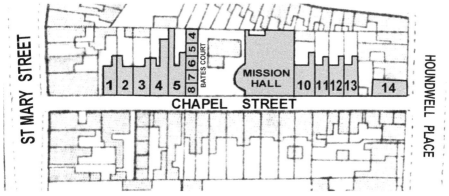

Nos 1-14 on the south side of Chapel Street in 1910. By this date only one section of Bates Court was standing. No 3 was the Oak & Ivy Inn, while No 10 was the Three Spiders pub.

tucked away off the main street. The courts, along with the rest of the street, were cleared away in the mid-1930s.

Chapel Street – South Side Nos 1-14

Nos 1-14 were on the south side, beginning at the St Mary Street end, then running back as Nos 15-31 on the north side from Houndwell Place. No 3 was once a pub named the *Oak and Ivy Inn,* which must have been one of the area's oldest hostelries as it appears in the 1836 directory. Edward Howell, a painter and a plumber, ran the pub for at least 30 years until the 1860s. It closed in 1905 and became a residence until the street was cleared. No 10 was also briefly a pub named the *Three Spiders* from the 1870s until around 1889. St George's Mission Chapel at one time housed a rifle range for the scouts until the First World War and stood steadfast until the area was cleared in the 1930s. A

Nos 1-5 Chapel Street in 1935, shortly before demolition, showing No 3 that was once the Oak and Ivy pub.

Corporation Wash House occupied the site until the Second World War. Bates Court originally consisted of eight buildings, but these were rarely included in the directories. Only Nos 4-8 were standing when the street was demolished.

Chapel Street – North Side Nos 15-31

The north side of Chapel Street was residential, with several courts tucked behind the houses that were accessed by narrow passageways. Graces Court had just two homes, but Newman's Court seems to have had just one three-storey house. There was a No 32 recorded back in the 1880s but that was possibly part of Bells Buildings.

A picture of Chapel Street taken around the time of demolition in 1935. This must be the north side as shadows are cast from the south. There appears to be a whitewashed passageway through the three-storey building that suggests these might be Nos 31 to 26 with the passage between Nos 29 and 30 leading to Graces Court.

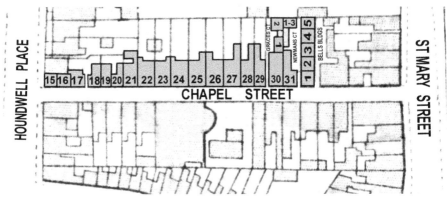

The north side of Chapel Street had 17 houses and a number of courts accessed by narrow alleyways.

This untitled 1935 photo shows part of Chapel Street that matches the buildings in Newman's Court as shown on the OS maps. The tiles on the right match those of Bell's Buildings that stood next door.

Another untitled photo of Chapel Street taken in 1935 where the buildings are certainly those of Bell's Buildings, a group of five cottages set back off the north side of Chapel Street. These dated from at least the 1840s.

Harrison's Cut

A little further north from Chapel Street was Harrison's Cut, which is still evident but much changed. It has never amounted to much more than a passage between St Mary Street and Houndwell but at its entrance from St Mary Street stood the home of one John Butler Harrison, holder of many

Harrison's Cut seen across the centre of this map from 1846 must have been a very pleasant place, with trees and gardens on either side.

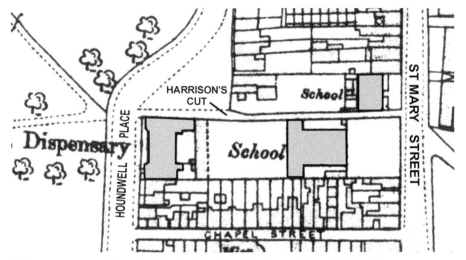

The area around Harrison's Cut had much changed by 1908, with a dispensary and schools replacing the former gardens.

civic offices in the town. He was related by marriage to novelist Jane Austen who, on her visits to Southampton, would probably have stayed there. At the rear of the house, on both sides of the cut, were tree-lined gardens, but upon Harrison's death in 1850 the house and gardens were sold off, the land being developed for boys' and girls' schools attached to the workhouse opposite in St Mary Street. By about 1880 a dispensary, vaccination station and relief office had been established at the Houndwell end of the cut, west of the schools, which were all demolished in the 1920s.

St Mary's Buildings, Pope's Buildings and Coronation Terrace

These three early Victorian cul-de-sacs at the bottom of St Mary Street were surprisingly not demolished as part of the 1930s clearance programme; instead they lingered on until the 1950s, but I have not come across any photographs of them in my research. All of them appear on the 1846 map, so were over 100 years old when they were pulled down.

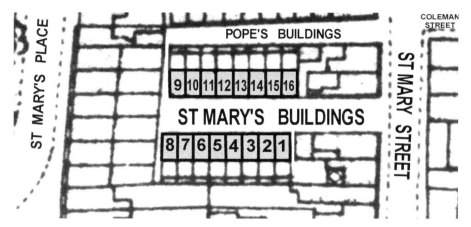

The 16 houses that made up St Mary's Buildings stood between St Mary Street and the rear of those in St Mary's Place.

St Mary's Buildings

St Mary's Buildings was a group of 16 cottages in two groups of eight, tucked away off the west side of St Mary Street with access between Nos 45 and 46. An alleyway next to No 9 led through to Pope's Buildings to the north. In the 1880s and 1890s, many of the residents were skilled men, rather than labourers, with a mixture of boot makers, carpenters, painters and tailors. Coppersmith William Osman lived at No 13 from at least the 1860s until his retirement in the 1890s, and the Hamptons were at the same house from 1920 until its demolition in the 1950s. The Pitt family inhabited No 12 continuously between the world wars, and the Ingrams lived at No 2 from the 1920s until the late 1940s. The Leach family at No 5 and the Simpsons at No 6 were there from the 1930s until the final days.

Pope's Buildings

Immediately to the north of St Mary's Buildings was another cul-de-sac leading off St Mary Street between Nos 47 and 48, opposite Coleman Street. This was Pope's Buildings, another early Victorian Terrace of nine houses originally. No 10 appeared in the directories from the early 1900s and seems

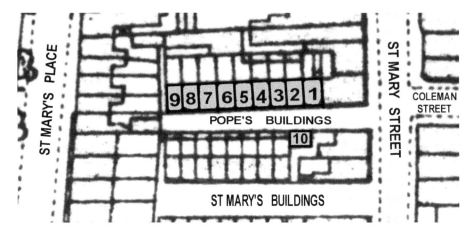

Pope's Buildings were originally a row of nine houses but later directories list a No 10.

to have been a building shown on the south side. At the turn of the century, there was an interesting mixture of residents, including watchmaker William James, stonemason Walter Stride and gas worker Albert Wyatt.

In the 1880s there were two resident blacksmiths, who were Frederick Coombes at No 2 and William Grady at No 5. The Coombes family were resident there from the 1870s to 1890s. Engine driver Alfred Foote and his family lived at No 8 from the turn of the century until the early 1930s. The Blake family were at No 3 from before the First World War and were one of the final tenants when the demolition came in the 1950s. In 1946, after the Second World War, Nos 1 and 2 were vacant for a year or two, while Nos 7 to 10 were all wartime victims and disappeared from the directories. Another final tenant was Samuel Ernest Payne, who had occupied No 4 since the war ended.

Coronation Terrace

The third of three early Victorian places, Coronation Terrace consisted of just five houses set back off St Mary Street, with access between Nos 52 and 53, opposite the Albion Chapel, all of which had fairly substantial

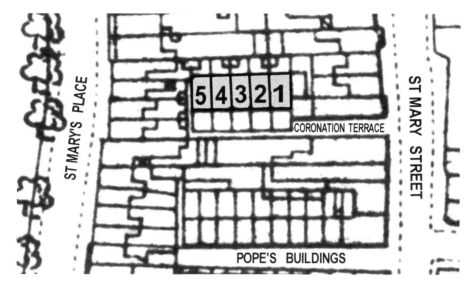

The short Coronation Terrace of five houses accessed between Nos 52 and 53 St Mary Street.

front gardens in comparison to their tiny back yards. The maps indicate that the buildings were somewhat larger than their neighbours in Pope's and St Mary's Buildings.

Although much older, Coronation Terrace was not deemed worthy of mention in the directories until the 1860s. Joseph Conroy was making shoes at No 3 from then until the 1880s. The Jocelyn family had moved in to that address by the 1890s and remained there until the very end. James Norris was another long-term resident at No 4 from the early 1900s until World War Two, after which Henry Bellows saw out the final years there. No 5 does not appear after the war so was a likely casualty of the bombing.

St Mary's Place

In their time, the properties along St Mary's Place must have been highly desirable, with uninterrupted views across to the Hoglands cricket grounds. They dated from at least the 1840s but were well past salvation by the time of the 1940s bombing and most had been removed by the end of the war, after which the building of the Kingsway dual carriageway saw off the remaining few homes in the 1960s.

Running north to south from South Front to Houndwell Place, and parallel to St Mary Street, the early residents look to have been a cut above the labouring classes in the houses behind them. In the 1840s and 1850s the locals were mainly professional or skilled people such as clerks, coach makers, joiners, tailors, printers, insurance agents and school teachers etc. There was also a fair sprinkling of 'Gentlemen' who had their independent means of income.

The number series ran from 1 to 40 but the final three, near Harrison's Cut, were once Nos 1-3 and listed separately. There were also two cottages off Kingsland Square that were included in the early directories. These were Nos 1 and 2 St Mary's Cottage. No 2 was also known as Slate Cottage, but both cottages disappeared in the 1870s.

Mrs M Young, also known as Charlotte, lived in No 1 St Mary's Cottage in the 1840s and 1850s until her tenancy was taken up by coach builder Richard Callaway. No 2 (Slate Cottage) was home to various occupants, including James Waterman who was a carpenter and joiner.

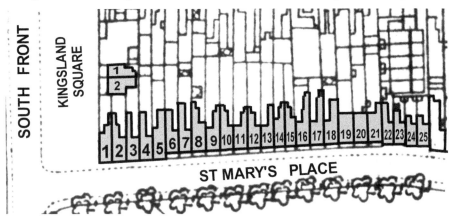

Nos 1 to 25 along St Mary's Place had commanding views across the Hoglands Cricket Grounds. There were also two cottages leading off Kingsland Square until the 1870s.

No 1 St Mary's Place was the home of plasterer Giles Bowditch through the 1840s and 1850s until boot maker George Chalk moved in and remained there until the late 1880s. Paper hanger James Mitchell was another long-time tenant at that address, living there from the early 1900s until around 1930. Arthur William Bacon moved in to No 2 about 1910 and was there until his home was removed during World War Two. Sign writer Frederick George Powell was one of the durable tenants, having lived at No 7 from the First World War until his house came down during the second one.

There were several ladies who were resident for lengthy spells. Mrs Harriet Eaton at No 9 and Mrs Mary Durkin at No 10 were there from the start until the 1850s, as was Miss Westlake at No 19 and Mrs Nancy Quirk at No 27. All were of independent means. It does seem there was very little turnover of tenants at many of the houses between the wars. No 12 was the home of the local Vaccination Officer Edward Ure in the 1880s. At one time in the 1930s, No 16 was a shop run by Mrs Annie Elizabeth Stroud and, on the 1846 map, No 34 is shown as the *Sailors Home* pub, with Jeremiah Hart as barman in 1853. Railway porter Isaac Bartlett was living at that address from the 1860s to the early 1900s.

Thomas W Spender lived at No 20 and in the 1850s was working as a clerk, but he was soon operating as an agent for various goods and services including the Great Western Railway and a purveyor of port and stout – a business he continued until the 1870s.

Robert North is listed as both Merchants Clerk and Gentleman during his time at No 38 from the 1840s until around 1870.

In the 1840s until at least the 1880s, No 26 served as a cut way and rear entrance to No 52 St Mary Street and Coronation Terrace. William Edgar Wray was living there from the early 1900s until the mid-1920s.

John Slight was another paper hanger who inhabited St Mary's Place. He was at No 29 from the 1860s until the early 1900s. Printer

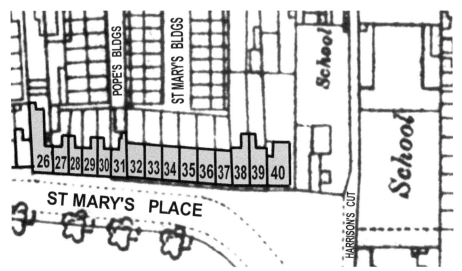

The southern end of St Mary's Place in the early 1900s, showing Nos 26 to 40. No 34 is shown on the 1846 map as a pub called the Sailors Home. The schools shown on the right were for children of the nearby workhouse (see Harrison's Cut).

Henry Allen and his family must hold some sort of local record as their generations were at No 33 from the 1860s right through to the end when their house was lost in the Second World War.

Looking north from No 25 to No 1 towards Kingsland Square, this great variety of properties in St Mary's Place were well past their best even by the time this view was taken in the early 1900s. Hoglands Park is behind the railings on the left of the picture (Dave Marden Collection).

Agent to the Great Western Railway Company,

For Goods from BIRMINGHAM, MANCHESTER and all parts of the North.

VANS FOR THE CONVEYANCE OF FURNITURE.

Goods forwarded to all parts of the Kingdom.

AGENT—

T. W. SPENDER, 20, ST. MARY'S PLACE,

SOUTHAMPTON.

Thomas W Spender advertised his many services operating from No 20 St Mary's Place. This one was as goods agent for the Great Western Railway in 1863.

SOUTHAMPTON LOAN SOCIETY

AND

Argus Life Agency Office,

No. 1, UPPER ST. MARY'S PLACE,

SOUTHAMPTON.

LOAN DEPARTMENT.

Sums of from £1 5s. to £15 lent at 6 per Cent. on good Personal Security.

FOR PARTICULARS APPLY AT THE OFFICE.

Mr. E. GODLEY, Resident Director and Secretary.

LIFE ASSURANCE DEPARTMENT.

Prospectuses, and all particulars relating to Life Assurance, may be obtained at the Office, as above.

G. H. BARBER, Agent.

N.B.—For the advantage of persons of limited means, and others, Assurances may be effected on the Loan principle, viz., by small weekly payments.

BUSINESS HOURS FROM TEN TILL FIVE.

The Southampton Loan Society gave cash to the needy in the 1840s and 1850s from its office at No 1 Upper St Mary's Place (later No 40) and you could borrow up to £15 if you had sufficient means and security. You could also take out life assurance as a precaution.

The Southampton Loan Society ran its business from No 40, which in the earliest days was No 1 Upper St Mary's Place where gentleman and secretary Edward Godley doled out the cash from in the 1840s and 1850s.

Hubert Hughes, Alfred James Pocock and John Campbell, at Nos 38 to 40, had seen out the final years there until 1940, with John Campbell having been there for nearly 30 years. After World War Two, only Nos 34 to 37 survived and Jack Wateridge at No 35 was the sole, and last recorded, tenant in the 1960 directory. From the mid-1950s the Surplus Trading Company occupied the space that was once Nos 21 to 25 and from 1960 the Stoner Motor Company were neighbours at Nos 27 to 33, while Southampton Art College had their printing department on the site of No 38.

Chapter 2

Grove Street and Bevois Street

In contrast to the cheerless environment to the west of St Mary Street, the later houses leading off the opposite side might have seemed quite splendid, being mostly arranged in open terraces, but still with the odd cluttered court. Grove Street and Bevois Street were two of the primary thoroughfares serving the area, with Bevois Street being part of a major route from the town to the wharves on the River Itchen via South Front and Longcroft Street. Grove Street provided a natural entry to Golden Grove from Chapel Road, meeting Bevois Street at its northern end.

Apart from St Mary Street, in the early days Grove Street was one of the longest and probably the most populated of all those that feature in this book. With over 100 dwellings, some of which were in courts off the main street, along with the usual pubs, shops and small business premises, it was certainly a busy place. I had omitted it from my previous book on the Chapel area because, although it began at Chapel Road, it was really part of the St Mary's area, leading through Golden Grove to Bevois Street and beyond. The 1846 map shows its buildings well established, with both sides of the street fully occupied.

Like many of the old streets in this part of town, Grove Street had its share of pubs and beer houses over the years, but I must admit, drink wise, it was unknown territory to me as most had gone by the time I had come of age, although many of the buildings were familiar to me as my little legs carried me the length of this long road on my way to Ascupart Junior School (now renamed St Mary's).

Grove Street

As always, with these old streets, the numbering system changed several times over the years, leading to some confusion as to what and who was where, but Grove Street is 'reasonably' straightforward, though there are a couple of grey areas. In fact this was one of the few streets to retain its up and down numbers, rather than be switched to odds and evens, until it disappeared in the early 1960s and the City College now occupies most of its former course.

Grove Street – West Side Albert Cottages 1-2

Generally, the numbers began at Chapel Road, heading up the west side up to Bevois Street and then back down the other side. The first buildings we find are the two Albert Cottages. Built around the turn of the century, they lasted until the street came down in the 1960s. The Riggs family at No 1 were there

The two Albert Cottages stood at the bottom of Grove Street near Chapel Road and were home to two long-term residents.

from the early 1900s until the Second World War, and the Frasers, next door in No 2, were resident from the same time but remained until the 1950s.

Grove Street – West Side Nos 1-25

The rest of the street had been in place by the 1840s and next we have Nos 1-11 where, at No 1, James Andrew was in residence from 1843

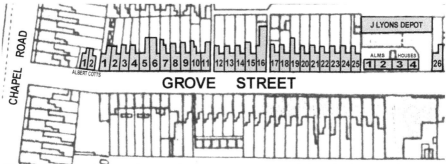

The west side of Grove Street showing Nos 1-25 and the almshouses that became Norfolk Cottages. No 16 was the Grove Inn and the shop at No 25 once sold beer.

Nos 2-5 Grove Street.

Nos 6-9 Grove Street with No 6 on the left having been a grocery shop for most of its time before World War Two.

Nos 9 to 12 Grove Street with St Mary's Church in the background.

until the 1880s, with the Blow family at No 3 over a similar period. Henry William Manley was then at No 3 from the early 1900s until after the Second World War, and the Cross family were at No 5 from before the war until the street was demolished.

No 6 was a grocer's shop for most of its existence, run by the Hamptons and then the Pearcys for most of the pre-war years, but one earlier family of shopkeepers at that address were the Whitelys, where William John Whitely was once a gun maker back in the 1880s. The Bree family inhabited No 10 from the 1850s until the 1920s while dairyman Charles Tubbs and his brood lived at No 11 and were one of the street's earliest tenants, appearing in the directories from 1839 until the 1860s.

Between Nos 11 and 12 was an alley that led to Short Street (previously known as Church Street) and Golden Grove. Blacksmith Benjamin Budden was one of the original street tenants back in 1836

Grove Street Nos 18 and 19 were left isolated after wartime bombing.

and his family occupied No 12 for 30 years, while Nos 13, 14 and 15 disappeared after the Blitz of 1940.

No 16 survived until the end. This was the *Grove Inn* pub, dating back to the 1850s, which had a change of name in 1879 when it became the *Oddfellows Arms* before reverting to its original name around 1900. Originally owned by Crowleys Alton Brewery, it was taken over by Watneys in 1947. Last orders came when the pub was demolished in June 1963. Alongside the *Grove Inn* was another cut way leading though to Golden Grove. Nos 17 to 25 were greatly reduced during the wartime bombing and only Nos 18 and 19 survived until the end. No 25 was a grocery shop from the 1840s, mainly under the Arnold family, who also sold beer there in the 1850s. Tom Topp moved in during the early 1900s and ran it as a butcher's shop. It was then a fried fish shop in 1912.

The old Almshouses in Grove Street were renamed Norfolk Cottages, seen here in 1959 with the Lyons & Co depot at the rear.

Grove Street – West Side Almshouses – Norfolk Cottages

Between Nos 25 and 26 stood a row of Almshouses, built in 1831 to replace others dating back to 1564 that had been demolished when the nearby workhouse was built. The early maps show seven dwellings but they had been reduced to four by the 1930s. These survived as Norfolk Cottages and were among the last buildings to remain in the street in the 1960s. A depot for caterers J Lyons & Co was built at the rear of the cottages in about 1930 and lasted a little while longer.

Grove Street – West Side Nos 26-42

None of Nos 26 to 42 survived the Second World War. Mr John Wheeler and his family at No 39 were among those made homeless. He had lived there but a few years, while other long-standing residents such as the Eyers at No 29, the Knights at No 31, and the Barrows at Nos 32 and 33 had been there for generations.

Between Nos 39 and 40 was an alleyway leading to Cumberland Street. No 40 was originally a pub named the *Bricklayers Arms* owned by the Edwards Botley Brewery back in the 1840s. In the 1860s it had

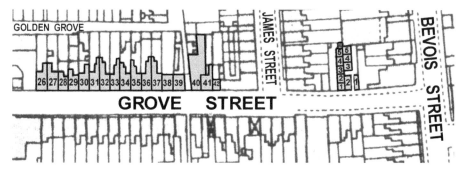

Nos 26-42 were lost in the wartime bombing and the Courts near Bevois Street had already gone by 1935. No 40 was the Malt Shovel pub, where there was a passageway through to Golden Grove and Cumberland Street.

Mr John Wheeler in the doorway of his home at No 39 Grove Street, which was one of many properties lost to wartime bombing.

Nos 39-42 Grove Street from an old newspaper cutting in 1929 shows the garage doors next to No 42. On the left of the photo is No 39, with the former Malt Shovel pub next door (Jim Brown Collection).

changed its name to the *Hit or Miss* but, for some reason, closed in the 1880s and became a greengrocers run by John Dawson. However, a decade later it was back in business, this time renamed as the *Malt Shovel,* but time was called when the brewery was refused a licence in 1909 and it became a shop once again until that section of the street fell victim to wartime bombs.

A garage, adjacent to No 42 Grove Street, was the scene of a gruesome murder by hammer blows. The body of Vivian Messiter was found there under a pile of wooden crates on 10 January 1929. His killer, William Henry Podmore, was traced, arrested and hanged.

Grove Street – Goddard's and Tucker's Courts

At the top end of Grove Street were a number of small homes tucked away between James Street and Bevois Street. These were Goddard's Court and Tucker's Court, the latter was later known as Grove Street Cottages.

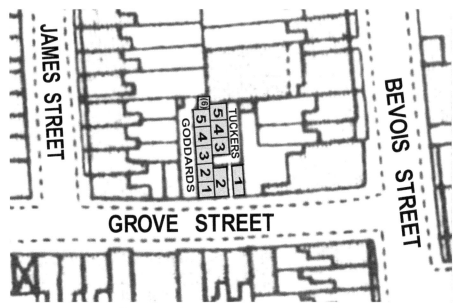

The small courts off the top of Grove Street were originally known as Goddard's and Tucker's Buildings, dating from around 1840 and lasting until 1935. The small building at the end of Goddard's Court might have been No 6 at one time.

Nos 1-5 Goddard's Cottages seen shortly before demolition in 1935.

Nos 3-5 Grove Street Cottages were formerly Tucker's Court. No 2 is on the left of the picture. The cottages stood back to back with those in Goddard's Court.

The flats that replaced Goddard's Court and Grove Street Cottages in 1935. The building nearest the camera belonged to the sausage factory of J H Dewhurst.

Goddard's and Tucker's dated back to the 1840s when Goddard's consisted of six cottages, but it had been reduced to five by 1920. Tucker's Court was entered via a passage off Grove Street between Nos 1 and 2, leading to another three homes. All the cottages stood until 1935 when they were replaced by a block of flats. After the war, J H Dewhurst established a sausage factory next door to the flats which became No 43A.

Grove Street – East Side Nos 43-69

Dock labourer Robert Lock lived in No 43 from the 1880s until the 1920s, while the Wrixon family were next door at No 44 from the early 1900s until the post-war years. No 45 was always a grocery shop from way back in the 1840s when Bradley Wiggins ran it, through to William Hutchings time in the 1930s. It had become a private residence and a builder's store by the time it was destroyed by bombing during the war. Moorgreen Metal industries were on the site during the 1950s.

No 46 suffered a similar wartime demise. From the 1880s it was mostly a dairy with the odd spells as a wood or coal yard at times. Charles Sturges was the proprietor from those days until around 1920 when Southern Counties Dairies moved in. Sturges also operated next door at Nos 47 and 48 where he ran a furniture removal business until

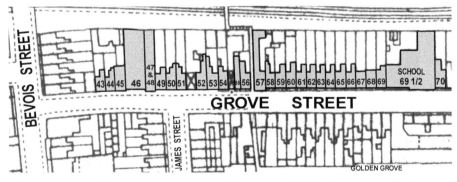

The east side of Grove Street showing Nos 43 to 69. No 52 was the Rink Tavern and No 57 was the United Britons pub which stood on the corner of an alley that was part of the Golden Grove Footway.

Nos 43 and 44 Grove Street in the return numbers running down the east side from Bevois Street.

coal merchant Frederick Hollick took over and the yard was also lost in the war.

The Second World War accounted for Nos 49 to 56, where No 52 was once a pub. Back in the 1860s it was the *Somerset Arms*, run by Jane Lucas, whose husband Thomas ran the nearby *United Britons* at No 57. The *Somerset* changed its name briefly to the *Cabman's Arms* in the early 1870s before becoming the *Rink Tavern*, but it closed in 1925 and became a residence. No 53 was another grocery shop after being a marine stores in its earlier days until the turn of the century.

The *United Britons* at No 57 began back in 1840s as the *True Briton* but changed its name soon afterwards. Jane Lucas, who had previously been hostess of the nearby *Somerset Arms*, took over from husband Thomas around 1870 and remained in charge for over a decade. From then on the pub appears to have been run by a succession of landladies until Walter Farwell arrived during the First World War. Previously owned by Ashby's Eling Brewery, the pub was taken over by Strongs

Pupils at Grove Street School in the early 1900s.

of Romsey in 1922 before it closed in 1924. It was then a fried fish shop before becoming a sweetshop under Vincenza Pantane around

Nos 57-60 Grove Street. No 57 on the left was once the United Britons pub.

Nos 61-64 Grove Street.

Nos 65-69 Grove Street.

1930. After the Second World War it became a general store run by the Patterson family until demolition in 1960.

Nos 56 and 57 stood either side of an alleyway that was originally part of an early right of way known as the Golden Grove Footway, which ran from Marine Parade to Golden Grove. When the railway to the terminus station arrived in 1839 a footbridge was built over it to maintain the old walkway, which continued on to Golden Grove through another passage between Nos 39 and 40. Nos 58 to 69 survived the war, with the Hintons at No 64 having been there from the 1880s until the 1940s.

The quaintly numbered 69½ was St Mary's School from the 1850s until the mid-1930s when Westlakes Sacks took over the site. They became West of England Sacks in the 1950s until making way for the Southampton Technical College in 1960.

Grove Street – East Side Nos 70-96

Nos 70 and 71 were wartime victims but Nos 73-81 survived the conflict. No 74 became a shop in the 1880s run by Charles Daish and then for many years by the Bellows family, who were still there in the final days.

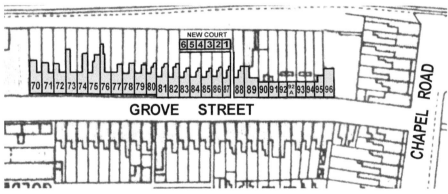

Nos 70 to 96 on the east side of Grove Street at its southern end near Chapel Road, showing the cottages at New Court accessed through the passageway between Nos 87 and 88. No 89 was at one time the Star Inn and No 96 was the Apollo Inn Tap.

Nos 73-77 Grove Street with the Bellows shop at No 74.

Nos 78-81 Grove Street with a gap formerly occupied by Nos 82-87 that were lost in the war.

Nos 88-92 Grove Street. A passage to New Court was between Nos 87 and 88. Second from left is No 89, which at one time was the Star Inn.

Nos 82 to 87 failed to survive the war and the Sims family lost their home after being at No 84 since the turn of the century. The Gates family at No 88 were there even longer. Having moved in during the early 1900s, they lived on through the war and stayed until the very end.

No 89 had an interesting history as it began as a pub back in the 1840s known as the *Star Inn* run by Scrace's Star Brewery, but as with so many old pubs in the area it lost its licence in the early 1900s and closed in 1905.

Grove Street – New Court Nos 1-6

Another hidden group of cottages was New Court, tucked behind the houses at the lower end of Grove Street and backing on to the railway line that went down to the Terminus Station. These six homes were also only accessible through a narrow passageway between Nos 87 and 88 Grove Street. They appear in the 1851 directory and lasted until 1935.

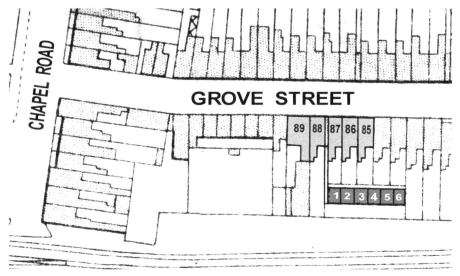

The six cottages of New Court were accessed by an alleyway between Nos 87 and 88 Grove Street.

Nos 90 to 95 were once known as Grove Terrace, which included a No 92A. My vague memory of visiting someone there tells me that on entering the small house, the front door took you directly into the living room and the stairs were behind a door in the opposite corner.

Grove Street's New Court was tucked away behind the main street. If the gentleman is standing outside No 3 in this 1935 photograph, he is probably William Jeffrey who was the final tenant at that address.

Nos 92 to 96 Grove Street. No 96 on the right was once the Apollo Inn Tap.

No 96 was once the *Apollo Inn Tap*, originally called the *Apollo Saloon* and not to be confused with the *Apollo Inn* on the corner of Chapel Road. *The Apollo Inn Tap* dated from the 1840s but had closed by the 1870s. However, it had a brief revival as a bar in the 1930s when it opened as the *Southampton Sports and Social Club*. Baron Brothers Upholsterers took over the site as No 97 at the beginning of the war and this was one of the last buildings standing in the street by 1970.

Bevois Street

Bevois Street took its name from the character in Southampton folklore and was perhaps the most important of those on the east side of St Mary Street, being part of the main thoroughfare from the town to the wharves at the River Itchen. Standing between South Front and Longcroft Street, it passed Aberdeen Street, Grove Street, Clifford Street and Melbourne

54

The last remaining section of Bevois Street with its drinking fountain at the centre, now known as Jonas Nichols square, viewed from St Mary Street (Dave Marden).

Street and spanned both sides of the railway level crossing. It was a major road with many houses, shops and pubs, together with the rebuilt Ascupart School on its route. Sadly, as with most streets in the area, it has all but vanished and only a short section at the St Mary Street end remains. That is now named Jonas Nichols Square after the builder who laid out nearby Nichols Town and the drinking fountain here is dedicated to him. It was previously at Six Dials and then moved to Kingsland Square before its current location.

Bevois Street – North Side Nos 1-33

The former No 1 (now No 4 Jonas Nichols Square) is probably the only original building remaining from the 150 or so that once lined Bevois Street. It was a shop back as far as the 1880s, in its time selling groceries, sweets, wool and then toys. No 2 was also a grocery shop, a hairdressers and a cycle dealers before undertakers R Hallum & Son based their stables there from around 1930. After the war the premises was rebuilt

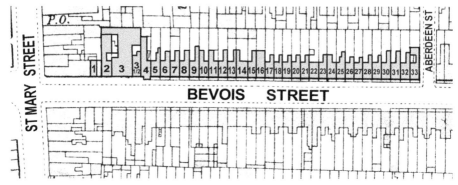

The north side of Bevois Street between St Mary Street and Aberdeen Street, showing Nos 1 to 33.

as a garage with a carpenter's workshop above and it is still maintained by the same firm.

Back in the 1830s, No 3 was a brewery, run by William Lock, which within a few years had become the *Bevois Street Tavern* run by his wife Rebecca until the 1850s. By the 1860s it had become the *Bevois Castle Brewery*, with the pub's name as the *Bevois Castle* until it changed to the *Bevois Castle Hotel* in the early 1900s, run by Philip Pomeroy who

Bevois Street Nos 3-6, with the Bevois Castle Hotel seen on the left.

C. ISTED,

Glass Blower,  Glass Cutter,

CHINA & GLASS

BURNER & RIVETER,

BEVOIS STREET,

(Four doors from St. Mary's Street),

SOUTHAMPTON.

An 1863 advertisement from the Isted family glass and china business, which was at No 4 Bevois Street for around 40 years.

was behind the bar until the mid-1920s. Owned by Gales of Horndean, it closed in 1964 and was then demolished, being one of the last remaining buildings in the street.

The rest of the north side from No 3½ (tucked alongside the pub) along to No 33 on the corner of Aberdeen Street were all residential, with the Isted family at No 4 from the earliest days until the late 1880s. Charles James Isted was a glass and china worker from the 1840s until the 1870s. The Plaskett family was living at No 9 from the early 1900s until the street was demolished, while Harry Blake was another long-term resident at No 11 from the 1880s until the early 1930s.

Bevois Street Nos 11-14.

Bevois Street Nos 15-19.

Bevois Street Nos 20-26 with the road traffic sign indicating the presence of nearby Ascupart School.

Bevois Street Nos 26-29.

Bevois Street Nos 30-33, with part of Aberdeen Street on the right.

Bevois Street – North Side Nos 34-50

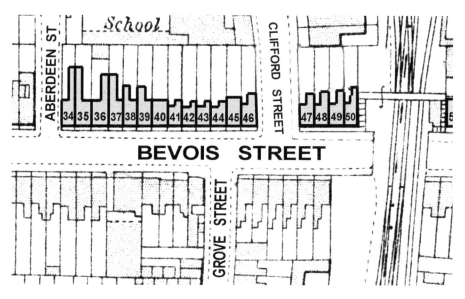

The north side of Bevois Street continued with Nos 34 to 50 between Aberdeen Street and the railway crossing.

Bevois Street No 46 looking north from the corner of Clifford Street. This was the only survivor in this section when Ascupart School was rebuilt around 1909, and it was home to Walter Pugh, who lived there for around 60 years.

Bevois Street Nos 47-50 were four houses that stood between Clifford Street and the railway level crossing, where the footbridge steps can be seen on the right.

The next section along the north side of Bevois Street from Aberdeen Street to Clifford Street was numbered 34 to 46 and all but No 46 were removed when Ascupart School was rebuilt and extended in about 1909. Walter Pugh had moved into No 46 in the early 1900s and was there until the end in 1960. Four more houses stood between Clifford Street and the railway level crossing. These were Nos 47 to 50 and the Lock family were at No 49 since before World War One until after the Second World War. Mrs Eade was next door at No 48 from the 1930s until the street's final days, but the McCarthy family were at No 50 for around 60 years from the early 1900s.

Bevois Street – North Side Nos 51-71

The final section of Bevois Street's north side ran from the railway crossing to Longcroft Street as Nos 51 to 71. To the east of the crossing were five buildings, Nos 51 to 56 – two of which were pubs. No 51 was named the *Full Moon* but another hostelry by the name of the *Three Tuns* had previously occupied the site before the railway was widened. The *Full Moon* was serving beer from the 1880s until it closed

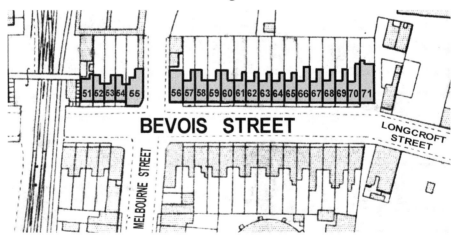

The north side of Bevois Street with Nos 51 to 71 between the level crossing and Longcroft Street. No 51 was once the Full Moon pub and No 55 was the Navigation Inn.

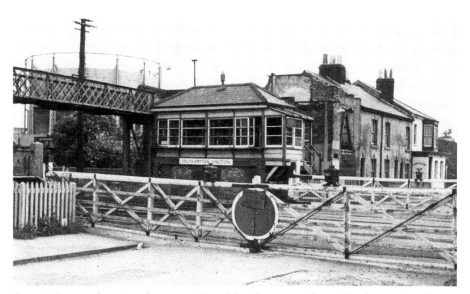

Bevois Street showing the east side of the former railway level crossing that closed in 1964, with Nos 51 to 55 beyond the signal box. No 51 was at one time a pub named the Full Moon and No 55 was the Navigation Inn (Dave Marden Collection).

in 1903. No 55 was also another pub named the *Free House,* until its name changed to the *Navigation Inn* in 1909, and it lasted as long as the street until around 1960. No 56 on the corner of the gasworks entrance was a grocery shop that had earlier been a bakery. It disappeared after 1940 along with the rest of the row between the gasworks entrance and Longcroft Street. Henry Switzer was at No 66 from the early 1900s almost until the Second World War, while neighbours James Hensford (at No 67) and James Henry Scott (No 68) were also there from the same time until their homes were destroyed.

Bevois Street – South Side Nos 71A-90

The south side of Bevois Street between Longcroft Street and the top of Melbourne Street was numbered 71A (or 71½) to 85, with 86 to 90 up to the railway crossing. Like its counterparts across the street by the gasworks entrance, there was naturally another pub to help slake the

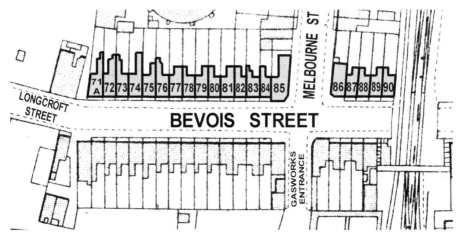

The south side of Bevois Street from Longcroft Street to the railway crossing showing Nos 71A to 90. No 85 on the corner of Melbourne Street was a pub named the Queens Head.

thirsts of the workforce. The *Queens Head* at No 85 was well established back in the 1840s. Once owned by Forder's Hampton Court Brewery, it was taken over by Brickwoods before it closed in the 1930s.

Nos 71A to 73 survived the war years but Nos 74 to 82 had disappeared by 1946. Until that time, the Moody family had lived there at No 75 since the 1880s. Likewise, the Warrens at No 78, the Pauls at No 81 and Scammells at 82 were there from the early 1900s. No 83 had stood the test of time with the Dear family there from before World War One until the late 1940s.

No 86 was a grocery shop run by William Manning since the 1870s when George Giles took over around the turn of the century. He was serving customers until the outbreak of World War Two. After the war the site was occupied by Longden Engineering.

Bevois Street – South Side Nos 91-105

The south side of Bevois Street, at the top of Grove Street, was numbered from 91 to 141 from west of the railway crossing to St Mary Street. As there are some interesting buildings along the way, I have split them

64

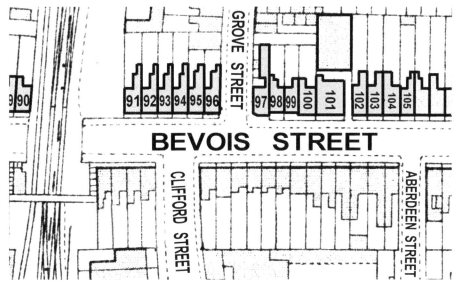

The south side of Bevois Street, showing Nos 91 to 105 west of the railway level crossing. No 97 on the corner of Grove Street was the Sailors Home pub. The workshops at the rear of No 101 were sometimes referred to as No 101A.

into three sections. Nos 91 to 96 stood between the crossing and Grove Street and all were residential except No 96 which was a corner shop. From the 1830s it was a bakery run by Henry Ireland until the 1870s. It then continued as such until becoming a grocery shop around the turn of the century, last proprietors of which were Pantenella & Son, post-war until 1960, doing a fine trade from the pupils at Ascupart School. William Gale resided at No 93 for over 50 years, from before the First World War until the street was finally demolished.

The *Sailors Home* pub stood at No 97 on the corner of Grove Street where former grocer David Biles turned to retailing beer in the 1840s. The Munday family took over from the 1860s until the 1880s before Edwin Hatch took up the reins in the early 1900s. Several other licensees came and went before the pub closed in 1962. Originally belonging to Barlow's Victoria Brewery, it was a Brickwoods house in its latter years.

No 101 had a yard with workshops at the rear, referred to as 100A. Back in 1863 John Smith was listed as a beer retailer at that address

Bevois Street No 97 was the Sailors Home pub that stood on the corner of Grove Street.

Bevois Street Nos 99-101. No 101A was a workshop and yard at the rear of No 101, which itself was once a beer house in the mid-1800s.

Walter Webb operated as a coal merchant from the early 1900s at 101 Bevois Street before taking up heavy haulage after World War One (Dave Marden Collection).

A bevy of beauties outside No 102 Bevois Street dressed for the 1936 coronation. They belonged to Joseph Henry Young, who ran a carting business from the rear of No 101 from the 1920s until the Second World War. The gates to the yard can be seen behind the group (Courtesy Tracy Faretra – granddaughter of Joseph Young).

Bevois Street Nos 102-105.

but its time as a beer house seems short lived as oil merchant Henry Bullen was resident in the 1870s and 1880s. The yard was taken over by coal merchant Walter Webb who lived at No 101 from the early 1900s, and he had become a haulage contractor by 1920. The premises and business had been taken over by Joseph Henry Young by 1925 until the Second World War. After the war, Herbert Robinson operated a taxi business there until furniture dealer William Spearing had moved in before demolition in 1960.

George Dixon at No 104 was one of the final residents, his family having occupied the house since before the First World War. The Lane family at No 106 were there even longer, having moved in during the early 1900s.

Bevois Street – South Side Nos 106-125

No 110 had an interesting history. George Walden was selling beer there back in the 1860s and 1870s when it became known as the *Fleur de*

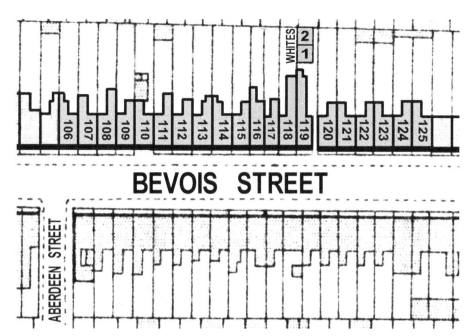

Bevois Street Nos 106 to 125, showing the two Whites Cottages at the rear of No 119.

Bevois Street Nos 105-109.

Bevois Street Nos 110 to 113. No 110 on the left was once the Fleur de Lis pub and became a sweet shop for many years afterwards.

Bevois Street Nos 114-118.

Lis under the Winchester Brewery. Its time as a pub lasted until 1910 when its licence was refused and the premises then became a sweetshop, where the Fullerton family were in charge from the 1920s until the end. Near neighbour Enos Parkes moved in to No 112 during the First World War and also remained there until the street came down.

By the time the street was demolished, the Swan family had lived at No 114 since the 1920s and music teacher Silvia Spacagna was at No 117 since before World War Two. Many others were permanent residents from wartime until the end.

Bevois Street – Whites Cottages 1 & 2 at rear of No 119

There were several homes in Bevois Street that were only accessible through passages from the main street. The two Whites Cottages stood

Bevois Street Nos 119-124, showing the passageway between Nos 119 and 120 that led to the two Whites Cottages at the rear of No 119.

behind No 119 and were reached by a passage between Nos 119 and 120. Like the nearby Tripley Cottages at the rear of Nos 129 to 131, they did not appear in the Street Directories until the early 1900s, but they did survive the wartime bombing and remained occupied until the 1950s when Mrs Pratt and Mrs Green were the final tenants at Whites Cottages.

Bevois Street – South Side Nos 125-141

Henry Meads and his brood occupied No 120 from the early 1900s and were still there after World War Two. Mrs Allen was next door at No 121 from the war until the street came down, as was Frederick Western at No 122. Another final resident was Arthur Davidson who was in No 123 even longer, from the mid-1920s.

One of the earliest residents at No 128 was ironmonger William Short until the 1860s when bailiff Philip Oram moved in. No 128 has an interesting later history. Having previously resided at Clovelly Road and Wharf Street, John Uriah Rashleigh, a carpenter and joiner,

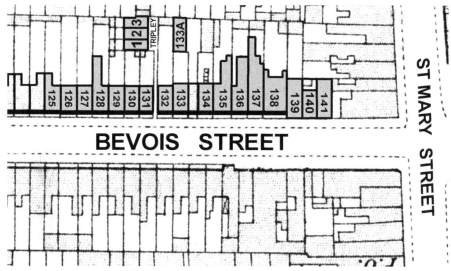

Bevois Street Nos 125 to 141, showing the three Tripley Cottages at the rear, with No 131 and No 133½, also known as 133A, at the rear of No 133.

John Uriah Rashleigh pictured on his doorstep at No 128 Bevois Street. He lived there from the early 1900s until World War Two.

The Crows Nest Club boxing team in 1938. Back Row: R Painter, J Barton, G Brander, F Sims, F Grubb. Front Row: D Pallett, H Rashleigh (Instructor), J Brander (Courtesy Marian Rashleigh).

moved to No 37 Bevois Street in the mid-1890s. By 1901 the family had moved to No 87, and then to No 128 in 1907. By 1887, the St Mary's Young Men's Association had founded the Crows Nest Club, which was an evening meeting place for underprivileged lads held at the Grove Street School. John's son Harry Cecil Rashleigh, born in 1912, became a member and

Boxer Harry Rashleigh in his prime (Courtesy Marian Rashleigh).

The Crows Nest Club Badge dated 1887 belonging to Harry Rashleigh (Courtesy Marian Rashleigh).

excelled at boxing, instructing others at the club to win many trophies. Harry had grown up in Bevois Street and attended Ascupart School. He went on to be a member of the school sports club and later the Southampton Amateur Boxing Club, becoming a local amateur champion by winning the Bill Blake Cup in 1932. Whilst at the SABC Harry became sparring partner to British middle-weight champion Vince Hawkins. In later years, Harry organised many sporting events and kept in touch with his former associates until his death in 1987.

J. W. GALE,

PLUMBER, GLAZIER,

House and Decorative Painter,

No. 10, BEVOIS-STREET, SOUTHAMPTON.

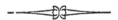

Beer Engines, Lift Pumps, Water-Closets, &c.—Prints Framed and Glazed.

PAPER-HANGINGS, &c.

WRITING, GRAINING, AND GILDING.

An 1851 advertisement for the skills of J W Gale who at that time lived at No 10 Bevois Street, which became No 131. He was certainly a handy neighbour to have.

No 131 was originally another No 10 under the early numbering system and, in 1851, was the home of J W Gale, who seems able to have turned his hands to almost anything, dabbling as a plumber, glazier and house decorator.

Bevois Street – Tripley Cottages Nos 1-3 at rear of Nos 129-131

Tripley Cottages were three small houses at the rear of Nos 129-131 Bevois Street with access through a passageway between Nos 131 and 132. The Cottages did not appear in the Street Directories until the early 1900s. They survived the Second World War but appear to have been unoccupied afterwards as no further tenants were shown from 1946 until their demolition in the 1950s. Another 'hidden' cottage was No 133½,

Bevois Street Nos 128-132 with basements that made them three-storey houses.

Bevois Street Nos 133-136. The gateway between Nos 133 and 134 gave access to the yard where No 133½ stood.

Bevois Street's No 133½ at the rear of No 133.

also known as 133A, that stood in a yard behind Nos 133 and 134 and was reached through a gateway between the two.

In the 1870s No 136 was where George Dean made shoes, but from the 1880s it was a tailor's shop run by Thomas Gannaway until Arthur Bergmans took over the business in the 1930s. After the Second World War it reopened as a general store run by Mrs Edith Glew and finally by William Baker.

No 137 was a pub named the *Boscawen Arms*. Back in the 1860s it had been a hairdressers run by Henry Stroud. It then became a general shop that sold beer in the 1870s before becoming a pub under Scrace's Star Brewery, with James Smith as landlord until the early 1900s when Henry Roberts took over and was still in place at the outbreak of World War Two. It was later owned by Strong & Co of Romsey when it finally closed in 1962.

No 136 on the left was once a tailor's shop and, next door, No 137 was the Boscawen Arms pub. No 138 was lost in the war and No 139 on the right was a fried fish shop.

The final days of Bevois Street as the south side is demolished, looking north east towards Aberdeen Street and Ascupart School (Dave Marden Collection).

No 138 had been a house rented by various seamen until Leach Brothers opened a saddlers business there in the early 1900s. It was taken over by Frederick George in the 1920s and was later one of the street's buildings that were lost to wartime damage. No 139 was variously a shop, then a hairdressers before becoming a fried fish shop run by Robert Willan in the early 1900s. James Turner took over the business in the mid-1930s and then David & Boucher after the war. It closed around 1960 as Perry's fish and chip shop.

Nos 140 and 141 was a pawnbroker's shop in the 1870s and 1880s. In the early 1900s No 140 was occupied by boot maker James Hinks, then, in the 1930s, it was taken over by Ernest Oxborough, who carried on the trade until the building was a casualty of wartime enemy action. A similar fate befell No 141, which was briefly a fishmongers and then a cycle shop in the early 1900s before becoming a sweet shop during the First World War, remaining as a shop run by Mrs Alice Collins from the 1930s until it was lost in the Second War.

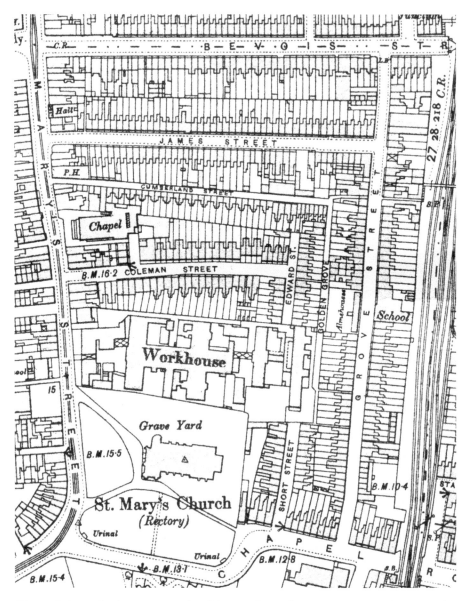

The tightly packed streets south of Bevois Street between St Mary Street and the railway line that ran down to the Terminus Station by the docks.

Chapter 3

South of Bevois Street

The area south of Bevois Street evolved soon after those that were to the west of St Mary Street as the industrial growth of the town expanded. Larger and more uniform than its neighbours across the way, the area soon filled with streets of terraces, connected by a network of cut ways and alleys. Shops pubs and small industries completed the tapestry of mid-Victorian life.

Golden Grove

Modern-day Golden Grove takes its name from an ancient footway that ran from St Mary's Church to Northam Farm, running parallel with Grove Street and having several other footways leading off it. I have no personal recollection of the street as it did not survive World War Two and was just a bare roadway in my boyhood travels to Ascupart School, but this narrow thoroughfare was still in place in the early 1960s until the whole area around it was redeveloped.

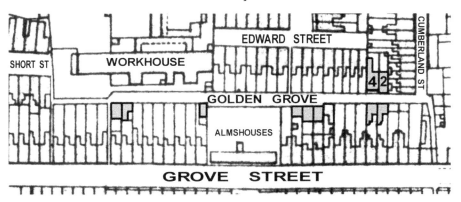

Golden Grove as it appeared in the early 1900s, showing Nos 2 and 4 on the west side. Other houses were on the east side, but I have been unable to identify them.

By the mid-1800s, as the local area was growing, a few buildings had sprung up along its route but it was never much more than a passageway between the rears of the buildings that backed onto it. Nevertheless, there were nine abodes, including a shop, scattered along it by the turn of the 20th century. As ever, the numbering was haphazard and it is almost impossible to identify individual buildings, except to say Nos 2 and 4 were on the west side and Nos 9, 11, 19, 23, 25 (a shop), 2A, 43 and 44 were on the east side at the rear of Grove Street.

There were eight residents listed in the 1860s with just seven in the 1880s, including three that were employed by the local railway. The Glasspool family were at No 2 from the early 1900s until World War Two, and Isaac McCarthy occupied No 4 from the same time until Albert Wyatt moved in during the 1930s. Edward Kennard was another long-term resident over a similar period in No 43. Mrs Brown ran a shop at No 25 in the early 1900s. By 1940 there were just three residents and the whole street had disappeared from the directories after World War Two, presumably a victim of enemy bombing.

James Street

Dating back to the mid-1800s, James Street, like its near neighbour Coleman Street, was one of the few to retain its identity after the redevelopment of Golden Grove, but that is in name only as no original buildings survive from the time of demolition in the early 1960s.

Running east from St Mary Street to Grove Street, it had houses on both sides of the street and retained its 'up and back' numbering rather than odds and evens. Having said that, there were several changes over the years as buildings came and went and, in all, there were some 90 houses.

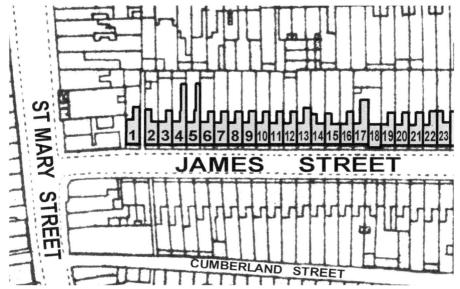

The north side of James Street showing Nos 1-23 off St Mary Street.

James Street – North Side Nos 1-23

No 1 was a detached house with an alleyway separating it from the rest of the terrace. Thomas Matthews and his family occupied No 7 from at least 1920 and were still there in the final days of the street. The Ruffells at No 10 were there even longer, living at No 10 since before World War One. Their neighbours, the Shears, were next door at No 11 from around the same time.

Over the years there were six pubs in the street but they gradually disappeared until there was only one left when the end came. No 17 was the *Clipper Arms,* which extended into No 18 around the turn of the century. It was originally the *Shepherds Arms* back in the 1860s but changed its name in the 1870s. Owned by Crowley's Alton Brewery it became part of the Watney Group before its closure in the early 1960s.

Bertie Price's family were other long-term residents at No 19, dating back to 1930 and the Couzens at No 20 were neighbours for a similar period.

Nos 1-3 James Street showing the alleyway between Nos 1 and 2.

Around the time of the 1953 coronation, outside No 3 James Street, looking east towards Grove Street. Anticipating the local street party were Barry Rodgers and Derek Smith with Chris Smith behind them. The taller girl is Sylvia Crowcher (courtesy of Derek Smith).

Nos 2-7 James Street were fairly uniform houses.

Nos 7-10 James Street.

Nos 11-14 James Street, where most of the front doors up to this point had a small porch roof.

James Street Nos 15-21 with the Clipper Arms at Nos 17 and 18.

James Street – North Side Nos 24-46

Continuing along the north side of James Street towards Grove Street we have numbers 24-46. The Squires family were at No 24 from the early 1900s until the outbreak of World War Two when Thomas Squires earned a living as a decorator. George Tanner moved in after the war and remained until the end.

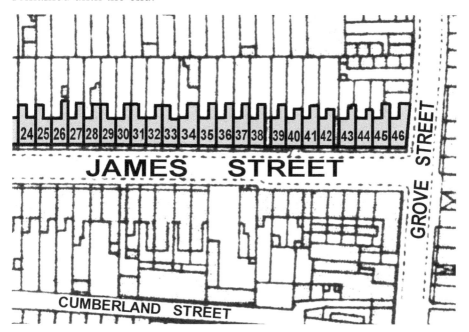

The north side of James Street, showing Nos 24-46 at the Grove Street end.

No 28 was once a pub named the *Kitcheners Arms* dating back to the 1850s when Henry Wright was in charge until at least the late 1880s. Owned by Strongs of Romsey, it ceased trading in 1910 and then became a residence where Thomas Walter Winter lived for the rest of its time.

The Hewlett family were living at No 29 from the 1880s until Harry Coker moved in at the outbreak of the Second World War and was its final resident. John Edwin Lewis was also the final tenant at No 30 where his family had lived since the early 1900s – Likewise, Charles Studd, nearby at No 32, was there for the same period.

James Street Nos 22-28, where No 28 on the right was once a pub named the Kitcheners Arms.

Nos 28-33 James Street.

Nos 34-38 James Street.

James Street Nos 39-42. No 40 with the large window was a greengrocer's shop, but prior to that it was a pub named firstly the Bird in Hand and then the King Alfred Inn.

No 40 was a greengrocer's shop run by James Kerley back in the 1860s, but by 1871 it was a pub named the *Bird in Hand,* with George Knight in charge. By 1900 its name had changed to the *King Alfred Inn,* with Charles Jelley behind the bar, but its time under its new identity was short lived as it closed in 1905 when its owner, the Winchester Brewery, was refused a licence. It then became a general shop until closure following World War Two.

No 46 had been a baker's shop since the 1860s when George Goddard was plying his trade, and by the 1880s it had become a general shop run by William Henry Jelly until the outbreak of World War One. It was then a residence until Nos 43-46 became victims of the wartime bombing.

James Street – South Side Nos 47-69

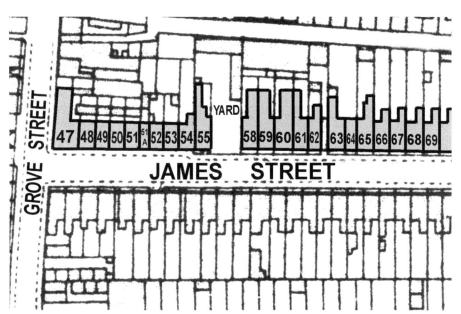

The south side of James Street Nos 47 to 69 with the Royal Exchange pub at No 47 on the corner of Grove Street. No 51A was a store and was the premises of builders Whitfield & Biles in the latter years of the street. The yard between Nos 55 and 58 belonged to the South Hants Motor Company after the war and No 63 was once the Avon Inn.

The Royal Exchange pub on the corner of Grove Street, showing the wartime damage before its demolition (Dave Goddard Collection).

Nos 51A-55 on the south side of James Street with the store at 51A nearest and the premises of the South Hants Motor Co at No 55. The gap on the left shows where Nos 57-51 were destroyed by wartime bombing.

Nos 58-61 on the south side of James Street.

Nos 62-68 James Street, where No 63, to the right of the handcart, was once a pub named the Avon Inn.

No 47 was a pub named the *Royal Exchange* that had stood on the corner of Grove Street since the 1840s. Owned by the Winchester Brewery, it had become a Marston's house by the time it was destroyed in the blitz of 1940. Like the buildings opposite, Nos 47-51 were destroyed during the Second World War, as were Nos 69, 70 and 71.

Back in 1870, a large timber yard and sawmill stood on the south side of the street where Nos 55-58 were eventually built. This was later the site of three cottages (named New Cottages) that stood in the 1880s at the rear of Nos 54 and 55. At one time there was a No 54½ next to 54, which later became No 55 when the site was taken over by the South Hants Motor Company repair depot in the 1920s and remained there until the street was cleared.

James Street – South Side Nos 70-91

No 70 was always a commercial premises. Back in the 1860s and 1870s it was a pub named the *Earl of Eldon* owned by Welsh's Lion Brewery, but it closed in 1878 when the brewery ceased trading. From the early

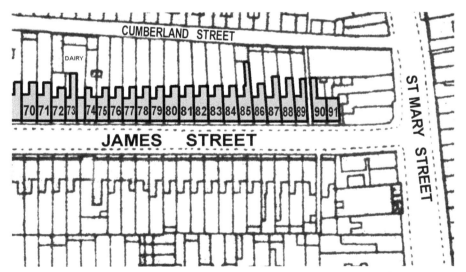

The south side of James Street showing Nos 70-91 running towards St Mary Street, where No 70 was a pub named the Earl of Eldon and No 73 had a dairy at the rear.

Nos 72-76 James Street, where a passage next to No 73 led to a dairy at the rear. The gap on the left shows where Nos 69-71 had been victims of the blitz.

1900s until the 1930s it was occupied by wardrobe dealer Henry Dear, and by 1939 it had become a greengrocer's shop run by Albert Pothecary, but that business was short lived as the building, along with Nos 69 and 71, were victims of the Blitz.

No 71 had been home to the Newman Family since the early 1900s, where William J Newman was a dairyman, possibly at the neighbouring dairy where a passageway adjacent to No 73 gave access to it at the rear of the house. It dated from at least the 1880s when Olive and Ann Stride ran it. John Henry Dorling took over in the early 1900s and remained there until the 1960s, but the dairy had ceased trading during the war.

The Stonadge family at No 77 were long-time residents from back in the early 1900s until the street fell in the 1960s. Similarly, Harry Corbin was at No 83 from the 1920s.

The final two houses at Nos 90 and 91 were separated from the others by an alleyway that led through to Cumberland Street.

Nos 77-80 in James Street.

James Street Nos 80-83,

James Street Nos 84-88,

Nos 87-91 James Street, where an alley between No 89 and 90 led to Cumberland Street.

Another view of James Street Nos 88 to 91.

Big changes came to James Street in the 1960s with the building of the Golden Grove estate. The framework of James Street Evangelist Church takes shape on the left (Dave Marden Collection).

Cumberland Street

Cumberland Street, running east off St Mary Street to Golden Grove, was quite narrow. All of its houses, apart from one, were on the south side, and, even by the standards of the area, were very small indeed. The north side was occupied by the rear of the buildings in James Street with a large timber yard and sawmill at the eastern end back in the 1870s. Nothing of the street now survives other than a few yards alongside the *Joiners Arms* giving access to the pub.

Cumberland Street – South Side Nos 1-16

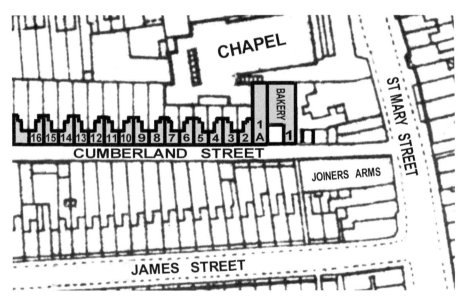

Nos 1-16 at the west end of Cumberland Street where it joined St Mary Street. Only the very short section alongside the Joiners Arms remains.

From the 1880s there was a slaughter house at the rear of 142 and 143 St Mary Street with access from Cumberland Street. Butcher Thomas Turner ran the business from the 1880s until the 1920s and the abattoir closed in the 1930s, with E Brown & Son being the final operators. From the 1940s, No 1 was a bakery run by George Edward Pope until the

Looking east down Cumberland Street towards Golden Grove.

street came down in the mid-1960s. Around the same period, Gookey's French polishers were at No 1A, which had previously been Conroy's ironmongers. According to the street directories, Nos 3, 4 and 5 and Nos

Cumberland Street looking east from No 3 (nearest camera) to No 7.

8 to 11 were unoccupied in the final years, while No 14 to 20 were lost to wartime destruction.

No 1A Cumberland Street was occupied by French Polishers W H & T Gookey from the late 1930s until the street was demolished in the mid-1960s. It had previously been Conroy's ironmongery works. Nos 2 and 3 can also be seen.

Cumberland Street looking east with No 8 (nearest) to No 10.

Cumberland Street, looking west towards St Mary Street from No 13. The open space is where Nos 14 to 20 were lost in the war.

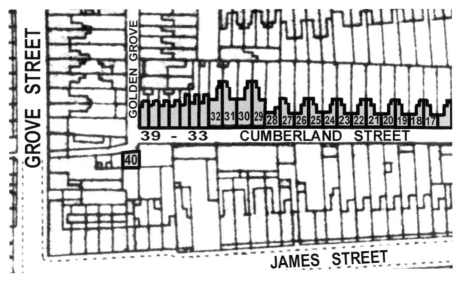

The eastern end of Cumberland Street, showing Nos 17-39 and the possible location of No 40.

Cumberland Street – South Side Nos 16-40

The eastern end of Cumberland Street looking east towards Golden Grove, showing Nos 21 to 24 and the bomb-damaged space where Nos 14 to 20 once stood. The 'temporary' corrugated cladding remained for around 20 years.

Cumberland Street looking west towards St Mary Street, with No 29 (nearest) to No 25.

Cumberland Street looking east towards Golden Grove, with No 30 (nearest) to No 35. Nos 36 to 39 were lost in the war.

Families seemed to like the street as many spent long periods living there. Boot maker Charles Barnes and his family were at No 21 from before World War One until the 1950s, and the Masters family lived at No 28 from the 1920s until the 1960s. At that time, the Jerrams at No 32 had been in residence since the early 1900s. Others may have seen similar long periods but for the war, which removed Nos 14-20 and Nos 36-39. The four houses numbered 29 to 32 were much larger than their neighbours, while Nos 33 to 39 were very much smaller and narrower. No 40 is something of an oddity as the later directories show it as being on the north side of the street adjacent to Golden Grove. Until the 1930s there was also a No 40½ occupied for many years by Henry Whitfield

Coleman Street

Coleman Street was fairly substantial and ran east from St Mary Street to the double cul-de-sac of Edward Street, where it had its own corner pub. The street also had a grocery shop at No 47.

Like many of the old streets, the house numbers originally ran consecutively along one side and back down the other, but this was later changed to the more familiar odds and evens around the turn of the century. On either side, Coleman Street had a couple of additions. These were Dickerson Place, which consisted of three houses on the north side, but a more secluded place was Coleman Court, a row of four cottages to the south, reached by a narrow passageway between Nos 43 and 45.

Coleman Street – North Side Nos 2 to 48

Nos 2 and 4 on the north side of Coleman Street were two houses between St Mary Street and Dickerson Place. William Ellis was a long-term resident in No 2 from the early 1900s until the mid-1930s. The

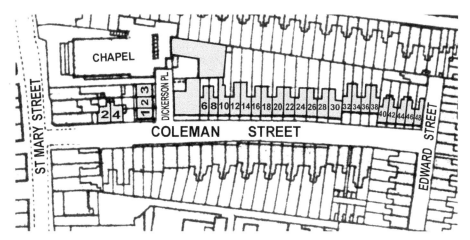

The north side of Coleman Street showing Nos 2 to 48 and the three houses in Dickerson Place.

warehouse on the corner of Dickerson Place was also sometimes listed as No 4 Coleman Street. Nos 6 to 30 ran east from Dickerson Place but Nos 8 to 12 disappeared during World War Two, where John Barnes had been at No 10 from the 1880s until the 1920s.

Nos 2 and 4 stood on their own between St Mary Street and Dickerson Place. St Mary Street's Albion Chapel towers above them.

The warehouse on the corner of Dickerson Place was occasionally numbered 4 Coleman Street. No 6 next door lost its neighbours Nos 8 to 12 in the war.

Nos 14 to 26 Coleman Street.

Nos 40 to 48 Coleman Street at the corner of Edward Street.

Nos 14 to 26 survived the war with some long-term tenants staying put for many decades. John Stubbs was at No 18 from the 1930s until the end. The New family were at No 24 from the early 1900s until the street came down, while the Leigh family at No 28 were there even longer, from the 1880s until at least the 1950s, but their house stood empty in the 1960s.

Nos 32 to 38 were a group of four, set back a little from the rest of the street, and Nos 40 to 48 completed that side of the street down to Edward Street.

Dickerson Place – Nos 1 to 3

Dickerson Place on the north side of Coleman Street had just three houses on its west side, with an industrial building and a store standing opposite them. The Forfitt family lived at No 3 for almost a century from

The three houses Nos 1-3 in Dickerson Place. No 3 was at one time home to the caretakers at the Albion Chapel seen at the end of the street.

the 1860s until the 1950s. Back in the 1880s Mrs Forfitt was chapel keeper at the nearby Albion Chapel in St Mary Street, which backed on to Dickerson Place.

For many years, the firm of R W L Delbridge had a corn store in a warehouse that stood opposite the houses. This was on the corner of Coleman Street and to its rear were buildings that originally belonged to a spice merchant. They were afterwards a furniture store, then a cable works, and its final occupants were E Mayes & Sons in the 1950s.

Coleman Street – South Side Nos 1 to 51

The south side of Coleman Street ran from No 1 at the St Mary Street end along to No 51 on the corner of Edward Street. Nos 1-5 occupied a site that was once the Albion Brewery back in the 1870s. This was at the rear of the *Albion Hotel* in St Mary Street. Charles W Watkins lived at No 33

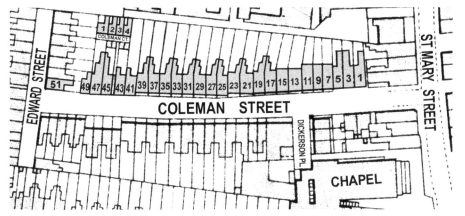

The south side of Coleman Street, showing Nos 1 to 51 and the four cottages at Coleman Court.

from the early 1900s until the street was demolished. No 47 was always a grocery shop run by the Holloway family from the turn of the century and then the Mawles from the 1930s until the 1950s. In the earlier years, it must have faced competition from No 51, which doubled as a grocers and beer retailer – the beer side of the business being a pub named the

Coleman Street Nos 1 to 11 (nearest) looking west towards St Mary Street.

No 23 Coleman Street (nearest to camera) to No 31. No 21 was demolished after the war and its outline can be seen on the right.

Nos 33 (on the right) to 39. No 33 was home to Charles W Watkins for around 60 years.

Nos 41 (nearest) to 49. Note the passage doorway, centre left at No 43, that led to Coleman Court.

No 51 on the left stands on the corner of Edward Street. This was once a pub named the White Dog that closed in 1932.

White Dog, which appears in the 1860s directories when Henry Sait was the earliest owner until the 1880s. The pub ceased trading in 1932 when Edward George Way was its final landlord, after which it became a private residence for its final three decades.

Coleman Court – Nos 1 to 4

Coleman Court was a group of four cottages that were only accessible through a narrow passage between Nos 43 and 45 Coleman Street, leading through an equally tight alley before reaching the yard where the houses stood. Coleman Court first appears in the directories of the 1880s and had disappeared shortly before World War Two.

The map shows the cottages and entrance passage between Nos 43 and 45 Coleman Street, and the first photo shows Nos 1 and 2 while the second looks from the alleyway towards Nos 3 and 4.

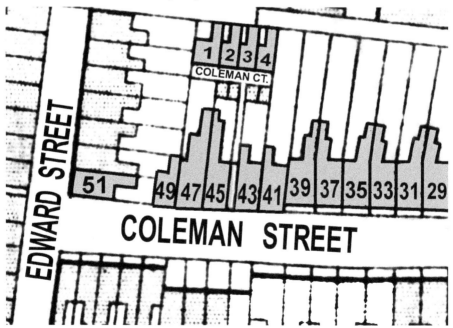

The four 'hidden' cottages that made up Coleman Court, which was only accessible through a narrow passageway between Nos 43 and 45 Coleman Street.

Nos 1 and 2 Coleman Court, which were two of four cottages off Coleman Street.

Nos 3 and 4 Coleman Court seen from the end of the narrow passageway that led to them from Colman Street.

Edward Street

Edward Street was a double cul-de-sac tucked away at the eastern end of Coleman Street in the shadow of the old workhouse (now the City College). There were 22 houses altogether and, other than access through Coleman Street, the only way out of the neighbourhood was through a cut way between Nos 7 and 8 that led to Golden Grove.

Nos 1 to 15 ran along the east side of the street, with Nos 17 to 22 opposite, while No 16 stood on its own at the north end of the street, tucked away in a corner as if it had been put there as an afterthought. There was once a street corner pub named the *White Dog* but that actually belonged to Coleman Street, though it was briefly listed as being in Edward Street back in the 1860s.

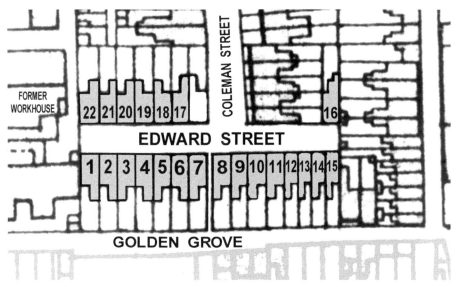

Edward Street where Nos 1 to 15 lined the east side of the street with a cut way between Nos 7 and 8 leading to Golden Grove. Nos 17 to 22 were on the east side, with No 16 tucked away on its own.

Looking west to Nos 1 to 7 Edward Street, with No 7 nearest the camera where the end of the cut way to Golden Grove is on the left. The old workhouse buildings can be seen in the distance.

Nos 17 to 22, again looking west towards the old workhouse. The corner building on the right is actually No 51 Coleman Street, which was the former White Dog pub that closed in 1932.

No 16 stands in isolation at the north-west corner of Edward Street. To the left can be seen the rear of the houses in Coleman Street.

The rebuilding of Golden Grove in 1965. From right to left are the remains of Coleman Street, James Street, Bevois street and Ascupart Street. Albion Towers straddles what was Bevois Street, and Ascupart (St Mary's) School is at the bottom right (Dave Goddard Collection).

Chapter 4

North of Bevois Street

The area north of Bevois Street was the last to be developed in the locality. The 1846 map shows it as being not much more than a large brick field with kilns and the main railway line along its eastern side running down to the old Terminus Station by the docks. The first substantial building there was the town gaol on Ascupart Street from 1855 and the rest followed throughout the 1860s and 1870s. These were, in the main, quite substantial houses, even if they lacked a decent back yard.

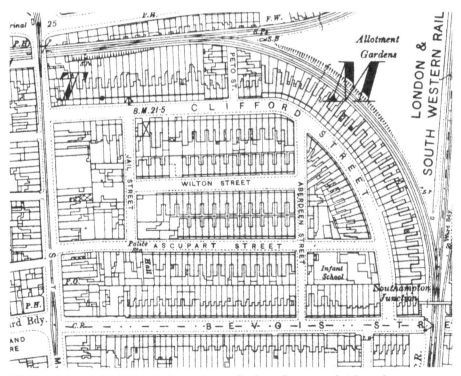

The streets north of Bevois Street were the last that were laid out between St Mary Street and the railway that ran between the Terminus and Central Stations. Although many had small yards, they were mainly more substantial homes.

Looking north across the old streets of Golden Grove with St Mary Street seen on the left running up to Six Dials. The long street across to the bottom left is Bevois Street. Jail Street is in the centre of the photo (Dave Marden Collection).

Ascupart Street

Ascupart Street, named after another of the characters in Southampton folklore, ran east from St Mary Street to Clifford Street, crossing Aberdeen Street on its way. In its early days, there was not much there other than the town gaol, built on the north side of the street and opened in 1855, replacing the older prison that was in Gods House Tower at the Town Quay. The gaol was considerably large, occupying most of the land bounded by what became Jail Street, Clifford Street and Aberdeen Street. It had cells for both men and women with its own laundry and extensive exercise grounds. The early governor was John Brewer, who previously held the post at Gods House Tower, and his house stood next to the main gate on Ascupart Street. The gaol had an annual turnover

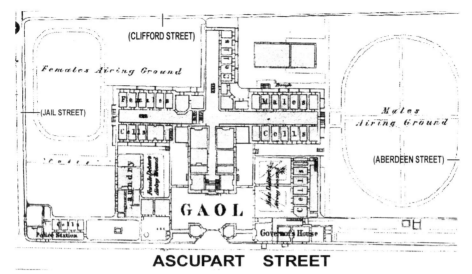

ASCUPART STREET

Ascupart Street gaol in 1870 occupied most of the northern side of the street, covering all the area that was later bounded by Jail Street, Clifford Street and Aberdeen Street.

of some 600 prisoners with a daily average of 50-60 incumbents until it was closed in 1878. It was long out of use and had possibly been demolished by the time of the 1897 map, where the male section had

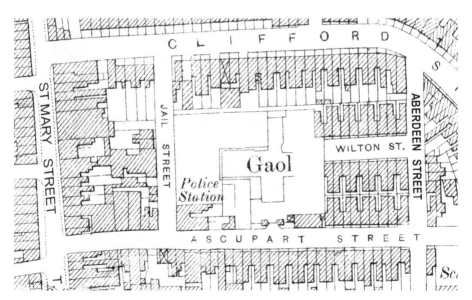

The 1897 map shows remnants of the Ascupart Street gaol between Jail Street and the beginning of Wilton Street, with the former governor's house still in place.

gone and had given way to the early houses towards Aberdeen Street and the beginnings of Wilton Street. At that time the former governor's house was still evident but that had gone by the early 1900s.

Ascupart Street – North Side Nos 1 to 59

Until the removal of the Town Gaol, the north side of Ascupart Street had very few buildings and hardly any housing until the 1880s. At the St Mary Street end was a lead and varnish works run by Neal and Sons, which occupied Nos 1-7 and lasted until the 1950s. In the 1960s, part of their building became a furnishing store and then an electrical wholesalers, but the upstairs of Nos 1-3 became the Oasis Bingo and Social Club in the 1960s and 1970s. No 9 was a house occupied by William Thompson from around 1900 until the 1930s. No 11 on the corner of Jail Street was a shop run by William Albert Bone from the 1920s until the 1960s. It was afterwards a ladies' hairdressers before the building came down and the whole block was rebuilt as flats in the 1980s.

A few more houses appeared as Nos 33-51 in the 1880s, but when the rest of the street was built in the early 1900s the numbering was changed, running as Nos 13 to 49 between Jail Street and Aberdeen Street, with Nos 51 to 59 further on before Clifford Street. As yet, I have not been able to locate where Nos 53 and 55 stood. The houses on the

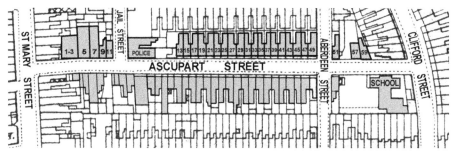

The north side of Ascupart Street in the early 1900s, with Nos 13-49 occupying the former site of the Town Gaol.

120

old gaol site, including those in Wilton Street, were virtually back to back with hardly any rear yards.

Long-term residents on the north side were the Turpin family who lived at No 15 since before World War One until demolition in the 1960s. The police station on the corner of Jail Street lasted until the 1950s. No 49 on the corner of Aberdeen Street was originally a greengrocers until it changed to a general grocery shop around 1930 and Mr Sheppard was the last shopkeeper. No 51 was the location of two enterprises back in 1912 when builder T J Pointer and coach builder Ernest Trimmer shared the premises. Trimmers had left by the 1920s but Pointers remained there until after World War Two.

Ascupart Street – South Side Nos 2 to 58

As with those opposite, back in the 1870s the only buildings of any note along the south side of Ascupart Street were concentrated at the St Mary Street end where wheelwright Edward Withey had established his business at No 12 and went on to be a coach builder at his workshops until the mid-1920s.

The first significant housing in Ascupart Street was built on the south side in the early 1880s, named Florence Terrace and numbered 1-10. Nos 11-22 were soon added, and when the south side was renumbered they became Nos 20-56, surviving until the 1960s when they were replaced by modern flats as part of the Golden Grove redevelopment.

The Mission Chapel stood on its own on the south side of the street in the 1870s until the houses were built around it. It then sat between Nos 14 and 16 before ending its days as the South Front Evangelical Church after World War Two until the 1960s. No 20 belonged to fruit merchant W J Baker back in the 1920s before being taken over by a Lead Light workshop from the 1930s until 1950s, ending as Athey's Engineering in the 1960s.

Nos 4 to 12 on the south side of Ascupart Street. No 4 nearest the camera was once a lead merchant's works and in latter years was a garage for Beeston's Undertakers. No 8 was Hampton's Confectionery store and No 12 was at one time Edward Withey's Coach Works.

The Burnet family lived at No 28 from the 1920s until the street came down, and the Poples were next door at No 30 for almost as long. Back in the 1880s, No 32 was the premises of cab driver William Underwood, as was No 38 under James Oliver. No 38 became Goddards Egg Merchants from around 1912 and Fiorento Gallone made ice cream there during World War Two until the final days of the street. William Bullen was at No 40 for three decades, as was Albert Bartlett next door at No 42.

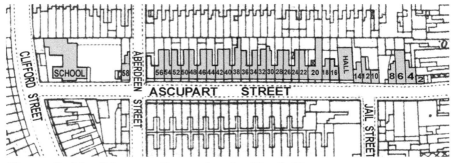

The south side of Ascupart Street, showing Nos 2-58.

The South Front Evangelical Church stood between Nos 14 and 16 in Ascupart Street. Back in the 1870s it was a Mission Chapel, then in the 1880s it was the Good Templars Hall and afterwards known as the Ascupart Mission Hall before becoming a non-denominational church in 1940.

Nos 18-22 Ascupart Street from right to left, with Athey's Engineering Works at No 20.

More houses on the south side of Ascupart Street with Nos 24-30 (right to left).

The south side of Ascupart Street with Nos 32 (right) to 38. Both were originally premises of horse-drawn cab and fly drivers.

Nos 46-50 Ascupart Street.

Nos 50-56 Ascupart Street with a glimpse of Ascupart School on the left.

A typical class of the early 1900s at Ascupart School.

No 58 stood on the corner of Ascupart and Aberdeen Streets adjacent to the school. From the turn of the century it was the premises of builder John Henry Dawson until it became a shop in the 1920s, for many years

No 58 Ascupart Street, under the shadow of Ascupart School, was once a builder's yard and then a shop before its final days run by a cable company.

run by the Wallbridge family, until after the war, when the Bradbury Brothers were spray painting there. The London Electric Wire Company was making cables there when the street's days ended.

Ascupart Infants School was built around the same time as Florence Terrace and lasted until around 1909, when it was rebuilt by the council as a Junior School and the building still survives today as St Mary's (Church of England) Primary School.

Clifford Street

Clifford House was a large Regency-style residence that stood approximately where Peto Street was later built. It dated from around the 1830s and was demolished to make way for Clifford Street, which sprang up from the 1850s onwards. To the south of *Clifford House* a large brick field with kilns extended down as far as Ascupart Street in the 1840s, this being the source of building materials to supply the huge growth of the surrounding area. Clifford Street itself sat inside the route of the railway line that once linked the Southampton Terminus and Central Stations. In fact, the curved section between Bevois Street and Aberdeen Street was originally named Clifford Crescent.

As with many of the old streets, the numbering system was haphazard in the early days before being revised in the odds and evens style in the 1880s, with odd numbers 1 to 139 on the north and east sides and even numbers 2 to 82 opposite. Unfortunately, unlike the neighbouring streets, it seems very few photographs were taken before demolition so there are not many illustrations of the wide variety of buildings that were there, but I do have a couple of photos I took from Albion Towers before they finally went.

The houses of Clifford Street across the centre of the photo as seen from Albion Towers in the mid-1960s, prior to demolition. It shows Nos 17-55 with the Clifford Arms on the right of the photo (Dave Marden).

Clifford Street – North Side Nos 1-47

Nos 1, 3 and 5 on the north side of Clifford Street included Alexander Thomas the boot maker at No 1, John Bondfields undertakers at No 3 and Youngs builders at No 5. Those addresses had all disappeared from the street directories after 1912, leaving just Nos 7 upwards. The Blake family were at No 7 from around 1916 until the street came down in the

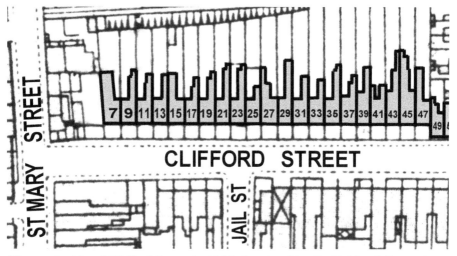

The north side of Clifford Street in 1910 showing Nos 7-47. Nos 1-5 may have been the small properties near St Mary Street, but they had disappeared after 1912.

Looking westwards from No 44 Clifford Street towards St Mary Street in the 1960s, with the Clifford Arms at the centre of the photo (Dave Marden).

Nos 43 and 45 Clifford Street were just two examples of many different styles that lined the street. Back in the 1870s and 1880s, No 45 was the home of William Goff, a school board officer.

mid-1960s. Likewise, joiner James Lloyd's family lived at No 15 from 1912 and also stayed until the end.

Clifford Street – North Side Nos 49-79

Moving eastwards along Clifford Street we come to the *Clifford Arms* at No 55 on the corner of Peto Street. The pub dated from the 1860s when Walter Edmunds was behind the bar. Belonging to Barlow's Victoria Brewery, it had become a Brickwood's house before its closure in 1968, being one of the area's last remaining pubs. The Moorman family were long-time residents at No 69, having lived there since at least 1907 until the mid-1960s when demolition came.

The Clifford Arms at No 55 on the corner of Peto Street was one of the last pubs to survive in the area when it finally closed in 1968. Nos 57 and 59 can be seen in the distance (Dave Marden).

Nos 49 to 79 Clifford Street were either side of Peto Street and included the Clifford Arms at No 55 on its corner.

Clifford Street – East Side Nos 81-139

Thomas Hampton was living at No 81 back in 1931 and continued to do so as one of the street's final residents. Nos 93-97 disappeared in

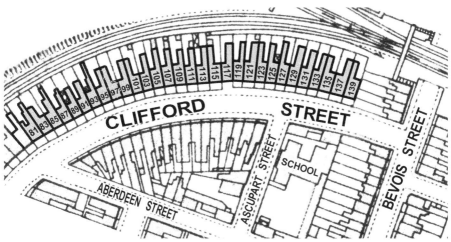

Clifford Street, where Nos 81 to 139 ran around the east side of the crescent from the end of Aberdeen Street to Bevois Street, following the curve of the railway line that ran between the Terminus and Central Stations.

Sunset over Clifford Street in the mid-1960s. At the far side are Nos 81-105 with a gap that was once occupied by Nos 93-97 until lost in wartime. The backs of Nos 48-64 can be seen, with Aberdeen Street running through the foreground (Dave Marden).

Nos 117-123 Clifford Street. The empty space on the left was created when Nos 107-115 were destroyed by wartime bombing.

The end terrace of Nos 133-139 on the east side of Clifford Street near to Bevois Street shows a fine example of some neat houses in that location.

wartime, leaving a gap in the street where William Prett had lived at No 97 since 1912. The same fate befell Nos 107-115, with William Dyer at No 107 and Henry Gee at No 115 losing the houses that had been their homes since before World War One.

Clifford Street – South Side Nos 4-46

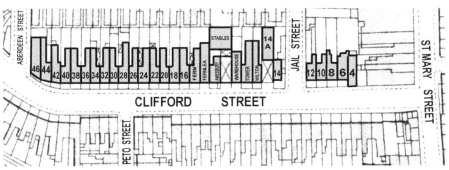

The south side of Clifford Street from Aberdeen Street to St Mary Street, showing Nos 4 to 46. No 6 was once named Rose Cottage and No 14 was Myrtle Cottage in the past.

In the 1840s, at the St Mary Street end, were two cottages named *Clifford* and *Albion*. These were gone by the 1870s as the street developed, and on the south side of the street No 6 was named *Rose Cottage*, with No 14 on the corner of Jail Street being *Myrtle Cottage*. When demolition came, No 6 had been the home of Samuel How since around 1930 and Mrs Baker had been in No 12 since the war ended.

Between Nos 14 and 16 were several named properties. These were *Wilton House, Tower House, Amesbury House, Fernlea* and *Fern Cottage*. Nos 18 to 42 were also named. In sequence, they were: *Hercules House, Mansfield Cottage, Brooklyn House, Waterloo House, Cedar Cottage, Walcot House, Landport Cottage, Monckton House, Trent Cottage, Lebanon Cottage, Dale Cottage, Oak Cottage* and *Valentina Cottage*, all sounding rather grand.

At the rear of No 14 stood 14A, which at one time in the 1930s was the premises of Ernest L Summers who made fireplaces and later moved to the bottom of St Mary Street. Prior to World War Two it became a garage run by Frank Nash, and after the war it was taken up by taxi firm Clifford Cabs until the 1960s. Between *Tower House* and *Amesbury House* was an entrance to what were originally stables run by Charles Sturges from the early 1900s until taken over as a motor garage by various owners from the 1920s until the outbreak of war. Adjacent was a brass foundry run by Drysdall Brothers from the early 1900s until around 1950. Founder Edward William Drysdall had been a gas fitter back in the 1880s.

No 46 on the corner of Aberdeen Street was originally a greengrocer's shop run by Richard Hardy back in the 1870s, and a decade later he was selling beer. The shop was taken over by his son David in the 1880s and he remained a beer retailer until about 1925 when Alice Perry took charge. Through the 1930s it became just a residence until William Good resumed the beer trade at the outbreak of war and, when the war

A sorrowful sight of No 46 Clifford Street, which ended its days as an off-licence (Dave Marden).

Dereliction in Clifford Street, but curtains still hang in defiance of the coming bulldozers (Dave Marden).

ended, Alfred Young ran the business until the mid-1960s. I cannot find any evidence this was ever a pub and it certainly never had a name, but in its latter days it was an off-licence run by Watneys.

Clifford Street – West Side Nos 48-82

Nos 48 to 82 were part of the original Clifford Terrace and earlier numbered 1 to 18. The Shine family lived at No 52 from the early 1900s when head of the house Joseph was a margarine maker. His wife Florence was there for the remainder of the street's days. No 56 was a baker's shop run by Henry Mould back in 1871; he had previously run a bakery in Melbourne Street. Henry was there until the turn of the century when George Fowler took over the business, but from 1912 the shop had become a grocery store, remaining as such until the outbreak of World War Two when Mrs Louisa Hampton appears to have been the final proprietor and the premises became a residence from then on. The Griffiths family occupied No 80 from the 1920s and were still there at the very end.

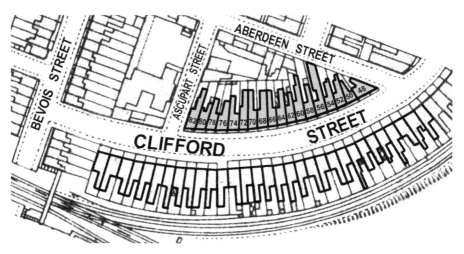

The west side of Clifford Street between Aberdeen Street and Ascupart Street, where Nos 48-82 were the original houses of Clifford Crescent and were numbered 1 to 18.

136

Peto Street

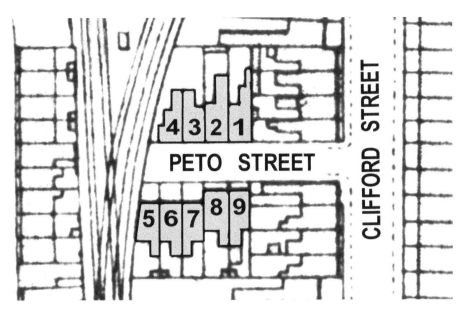

The nine houses of Peto Street with the railway junction at the end of the street.

Peto Street was short in name and short by nature. This small cul-de-sac leading north between Nos 55 and 57 Clifford Street contained just nine houses, with four on its east side and five more opposite. It was built roughly on the site of the former *Clifford House* and ended abruptly overlooking the railway junction between the main London line and that which curved around Clifford Street and on down to the Terminus Station.

The street was named after Samuel Morton Peto, a civil and railway engineer who was engaged to construct the tunnel that now runs under East Park to the Central Station and was opened in 1847.

Unlike many of the surrounding streets, residents seem to have been happy staying put in Peto Street for long periods until it came down along with Clifford Street. The McDonalds at No 1 and the Axtons at No 6 were content to remain there from the Second World War onwards,

This photo of the Clifford Arms offers the slightest glimpse of Peto Street on the right (Dave Marden).

The railway signal box at Tunnel Junction showing the rear of No 4 Peto Street on the left. The buildings on the right are along Northam Road (Dave Marden).

while the Franklins at No 2 were there from the early 1900s and the Lloyds at No 4 from the 1920s.

Jail Street

As its name suggests, this street was in close proximity to the town gaol and formed its western boundary, running north to south from Clifford Street to Ascupart Street, containing just two or three houses and a couple of industrial premises. Such was its insignificance, it doesn't get mentioned much in the early street directories, though it does feature on the 1870 map. Although it is no longer named, it still exists as part of the Golden Grove estate circular roadway.

Back in the 1880s there appear to be three houses with one of them named *Cancer Cottage*. Early residents were French polisher William Parsons and fly proprietor Henry Honeybone. Russell & Sons had a furniture store there from the 1880s until the 1960s. Builder James Pitt seems to have taken over Honeybone's yard in the early 1900s when house numbers 1 and 2 also featured regularly in the directories until

With a lack of photographic evidence, this is how I understand Jail Street to have been in the early 1900s.

the outbreak of World War Two, with the Cutler family at No 1 and the Rippingdales at No 2.

After the war, the former police station on the corner of Ascupart Street was used as housing until the 1950s, while Fraser & Son had a store at the rear of their St Mary Street premises.

Aberdeen Street

Running north to south between Clifford Street and Bevois Street, and crossing Ascupart Street, Aberdeen Street was also something of a nonentity. It had only five houses of its own dating from the 1880s and not much else, and it appears to have begun life as just the eastern boundary to the old town gaol. Nos 1 to 3 were huddled on the east side, opposite the end of Wilton Street, but No 4 seems to have disappeared in the early 1900s and was possibly where George Cawte had his coach painting business off Ascupart Street in the 1870s and 1880s. No 5 stood on the opposite side of the road on the corner of Ascupart Street.

The early tenants were mainly seafarers, while Alfred Moody at No 1, John Giles at No 2 and Frank Dawkins at No 3 were long-time residents from the early 1900s until the 1930s. The Brown family took over No 3 in 1940 and were there until the end came in the mid-1960s.

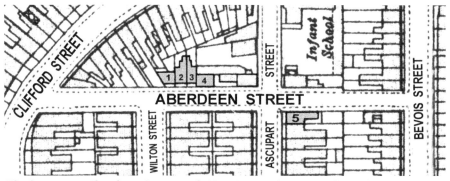

The houses in Aberdeen Street with Nos 1-4 on the east side and No 5 opposite.

No 5 Aberdeen Street stood on the corner of Ascupart Street. This view is looking south, with the houses of Bevois Street in the background.

The rear of No 5 Aberdeen Street looking north towards Ascupart Street.

Wilton Street

Wilton Street doesn't appear in the directories until around the turn of the century when it was no more than a few houses leading off Aberdeen Street to the east of the old town gaol site which once occupied much of the area to the north of Ascupart Street. All of the early Wilton buildings had names such as *Fernside, Southsea Villas, Albert Villa, York House, Fowey House, Alma House, Fern Villa, Heathfield House, Ada Villa, Somerley Villa and Manchester Villa.*

The 1897 map shows just 19 houses which would have included those named above, but, as yet, I have only been able to identify the names on the houses that were built later.

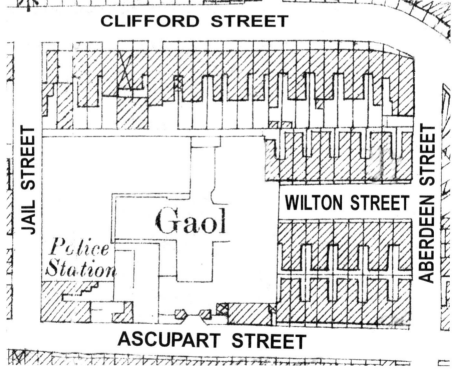

The 1897 street map shows the beginnings of Wilton Street to the east of the old town gaol site that had been long out of use by then. The prison Governor's house remained near its gate on Ascupart Street for some time afterwards.

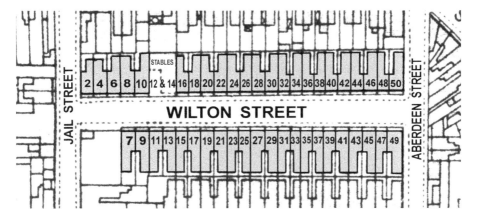

The complete Wilton Street as it appeared in 1908. Most of this area was previously occupied by the town Gaol.

By the early 1900s the street had been completed and totalled 47 houses, most with bay windows and attic rooms. The even numbers 2 to 50 were on the north side where Nos 12 and 14 were originally stables until the First World War when they were occupied by Charles Sturges, who had a furniture removal business there until the outbreak of the Second World War in 1939. In the final years it was the base for a minicab company. Incidentally, the Clifford Cab Company was next door at No 10, having been there since just after World War Two. Like the earlier houses, several had names. No 6 was *Kimberly House*, No 10 *Winchelsey Villa,* with *Clifford House* at 30 and *Wilton House* at 32. The Barham family were at No 6 from the early 1900s until the Second World War and William Jones and his family were at No 24 between the wars, as was William Brown at No 40.

On the south side at the Jail Street end, adjacent to No 7, James Herron owned some lock up garages from the 1930s until the final days. Another long-term stalwart between the two wars was Harry Lovejoy at No 15. The Wareham family were at No 17 for almost all of the streets history from the early 1900s until demolition. No 19 was *Florence Villa* where the Lockyer family were in residence from the early days until the mid-1930s, while James Sparrow lived at No 23 from the 1920s until the

143

1960s. George Davis was at No 49 from the early 1900s until after the end of World War Two.

Wilton Street is almost unique amongst those in this book in that it had no shops or pubs, not even a beer house. Also, it was another of the few streets not photographed by the town council prior to its demolition.

The end is nigh! Looking down from Albion Towers as empty terraces stand like silent monuments to a bygone era awaiting the bulldozer in the 1960s, with Wilton Street across the centre of the picture and the houses of Clifford Street in the background, where the Clifford Arms can be seen at the top right. No more doorstep gossip, children playing in the street or Saturday night sing-songs. Many of these houses were substantial buildings by today's standards and could have made fine homes had they been saved and modernised (Dave Marden).